Toy Glass

by Doris Anderson Lechler

Dedicated to Helen and Wil Feltner, La Vonn and Bob Rogers, Cindy Mangee, Joan and Tom Wood, and Ilene and Dean McCann—friends and fellow travelers; and to Marilee Mueller who introduced me to collecting.

APPLE TREE TEA

Do you recall the bygone days,
When all we had to do was play?
With tables, chairs and some glass,
China and granite, now amassed.
Who were the friends who came to play?
Could there have been a "Little May"?

We took our toys to the apple tree.
Kim, Kay, Frankie and Me.
We set the table, the bees did fuss.
All the ants came, as if by bus.
Frankie alerted the rest of the cast.
The memories roll in, and they do last.

Mother's rolls, fresh from the oven,
Resting on glass plates bought by the dozen.
The smell called "come" upon the air.
There were plenty of rolls, but not enough chairs.
Children gathered from all the close homes.
Each day is precious, now that time has flown.

Those times were not perfect, we must agree,
As I look back at the original three.
But what I would give for one more tea.
With special friends under that apple tree.

Doris Anderson Lechler

ABOUT THE COVER . . .

My childhood was sweet, thanks to my parents. This cover reminds me of that time.

Dara Cochran, our cover girl and my neighbor, displays a table full of glass jewels available to collectors of today.

Sitting in front of Dara, piled high with fresh, juicy strawberries is the Twin muffin stand. She spears the berries with an onion-skin-handled fork, a desirable accessory for collectors to locate.

Dara offers beverages from the blush Galloway lemonade set, the Petite Hobnail unit and the ruby glass miniature tea service.

The plump blueberries glisten in each bowl of the Inverted Strawberry dessert set.

Tiny cakes are displayed on various cake servers or plates.

All Dara needs now is Kim, Kay, Frankie and me . . .

Other books by Doris Anderson Lechler include:

CHILDREN'S GLASS DISHES by Lechler and O'Neill

*CHILDREN'S GLASS DISHES, CHINA AND
    FURNITURE (Vol. I)*

*CHILDREN'S GLASS DISHES, CHINA AND
    FURNITURE (Vol. II)*

MINIATURE NEWS newsletter

Forthcoming books by Doris Anderson Lechler, published
by Antique Publications, will include:

ENGLISH TOY CHINA

*FRENCH AND GERMAN DOLLS, DISHES AND
    ACCESSORIES*

ACKNOWLEDGMENTS

Working on this, the first of a series of toy-related books, has been an eventful adventure.

Each of the books will bring a different story. This book, which deals with toy glass and miniatures, will serve the collector of American toy glass best. It is, however, impossible for me to leave out the miniature glass lusters, epergnes, tumble ups and decanter sets which are more than likely European. Without their grace, I would like the book less.

My work was enriched by its collaborative nature. It joined the sensibilities and requests of collectors and dealers with the good eye of the photographers, the guiding rein of the publisher, David Richardson, and the hard work of several collecting friends and family members.

A special thanks is offered to: Collector Books for allowing me the use of several black and white pictures from my other books; Joyce Johnston who rescues me on many occasions and compiled the plates information this time; Seth Johnston who released her from work to help me with photography sessions; Bob Rogers who offered his expertise on Akro while his wife wrote to people asking for special things for the book and to both of them for coming to help in a snowstorm; Joan Wood who was kind enough to release a rare set right after she had received it; Ilene and Dean McCann for their help and support; Cindy Mangee whose enthusiasm and gracious generousness have helped so much with this publication; Blanche Largent who flew us to her house to pick up her glassware to be pictured here; Helen Feltner who took the time from her very busy life to ship important contributions to be pictured; Mr. Lynn Welker, a dealer and friend who always comes through for me; Helen Haskell who sent nice examples with the Rogerses for photographing; Judy and Dick Walters for sending items and giving general support with kindness; Tom Mosser of Cambridge, Ohio, for sending his new glass examples; Rosemary Ward who found two flare-top open compotes and offered one to me; Tom Neale and Glen Schlotfeldt who continue to supply me with treasures; Pegge Treager for special treats from time to time; to my new and wonderful neighbors, Dee and Doug Cochran and their daughter, Dara Cochran, who is our cover girl for this book; Jerry and Sandy Schmoker for allowing us to repeat some of their mug shots; and to Betty Dagenais and Nancy Lubberger for their plates.

I hope I have each person's contributions noted, but I'm sure I have some mixed up. Please forgive me in advance for this.

David Richardson is a special person who has taken this book under his wing and helped to make it work. I thank him for taking on this series of books.

Doris Anderson Lechler

FOREWORD

This carry-about book has several purposes, the most important of which is that it is a quick guide for collectors and dealers.

Another purpose in issuing this toy glass book is to show that we have indeed covered and pictured the patterns of toy glass available to collectors of today. Wish though we may, the fact remains that toy glass had a limited production life. There may be a newly discovered item here or there, but nearly all toy glass has been shown in some publication on the market. The scarcity makes our collections all the more dear.

The beauty of this quick guide to collecting is that the pictures are clear and uncluttered. We felt it was not necessary to put in six tumblers when a pitcher and one tumbler would do.

Groupings for this book are a little different than those in my other three books. The items will be shown in alphabetical order when possible, but within certain groupings:

BEVERAGE SETS

Included in this section are punch sets which consist of a pitcher and four or six cups; a water or lemonade set with a pitcher, four or six tumblers, and, at times, a tray; Stein sets have a main stein and four or six counterparts; tumble ups have a decanter, bottle or pitcher with a single tumbler fitting over the neck or, more rarely, inside the neck of the main container which is sometimes held by an underplate; decanter sets have a single main item with four or six beverage cups and, at times, a tray. Keg sets are rare in true miniature form, but one is shown in this publication from the Feltner collection.

BERRY AND DESSERT SETS

Berry sets, the ABC ice cream set, and the rare Fish set are shown as a group in this text. There are ten different berry sets displayed for study, each of which contain a main bowl, which resembles an adult sauce bowl, and four or six small salt-dip-like individual bowls. The ABC ice cream set and the Fish set each have a main oval platter and six small round plates.

TABLE SETS

There are approximately sixty different patterns in toy table sets discovered so far. Most sets are considered to be complete if they contain a covered butter dish, a sugar bowl, usually covered, a cream pitcher and a vase-like holder for spoons.

Sometimes, the four piece table set will have an accompanying plate, cup, saucer, mug or cake stand in the same pattern.

CANDLESTICKS

Single candlesticks are shown to save space. These items may be collected by the pair or as a single example of the more than thirty different styles made in the past.

PLATES

There are several examples of plates in this book. Some are novelty plates from important glass houses of the past. Others are toy cake plates which measure from approximately two to four inches in diameter. The Baby Thumbprint toy cake plates are shown with the open compote and the covered compote in that same pattern. Miniature counterparts of the adult line of ware measure from six to eight inches across and make nice display items with toy glass.

CASTOR SETS

Castor sets, while having several styles of holders with two to five holes, have a limited number of bottle patterns with slight variations in design or size. A castor set is considered complete when its holder contains bottles of the same pattern with original stoppers, caps or corks.

MUGS

A real variety of sizes in the mug line are shown in this publication with most of them being collected as part of toy glass history. The mugs are from the Largent, Schmoker and Johnston collections.

SANDWICH GLASS

Sandwich glass research by Raymond E. Barlow and Joan E. Kaiser in their *GUIDE TO SANDWICH GLASS Witch Balls, Containers and Toys* has yielded some excellent information for toy glass collectors. Collectors, in turn, have shared several examples of Sandwich toys in this publication.

AKRO AGATE

Mr. Bob Rogers has compiled a nice sampling of Akro Agate for this book. He has asked for examples from Dick Walters, Joan Wood and Helen Haskell. Bob Rogers has not only shown special sets from his own collection, but he and his wife, LaVonn, traveled to my home to help with that particular photographic session.

LUSTERS AND EPERGNES

While these items are more than likely European, they add color and interest to a toy glass collection. Many collectors consider them to be an important addition to their displays of toy ware.

CONTEMPORARY TOY GLASS

A sampling of contemporary toy glass is shown in this book. There has been no attempt to catalogue or document the progress of these sets. The reason they are included here is because they are a part of toy glass history and many collectors like to add them to their toy glass time line.

MISCELLANEOUS MINIATURES

This section carries the remainder of all the old toy glass accessories.

REPRODUCTIONS

It is worth noting right away that there is little need for concern in the area of reproductions.

In the first place, sets having reproduced patterns number

fewer than a dozen. The actual nine reproduced patterns seem like more simply because the sets have been cast in a variety of marketable colors. Generally, these colors are new to the toy glass realm because the past producers used little imagination when dealing out shades for these charming sets of glass. Amber, blue, green and the most popular, crystal, were the standard selections. Two patterns, Austrian #200 and Sultan, were produced in the popular chocolate glass. A few toy examples were produced in white or blue milkglass.

Out of sixty patterns in toy table sets, portions of only five have been reproduced. They are: Hawaiian Lei from Tom Mosser in Cambridge, Ohio; Lamb; Flattened Diamond, reissued by Westmoreland; Kemple's Tappan; and L.E. Smith's creamer and spooner in the Chimo pattern. Granted, they were produced in nearly every color imaginable, but they are also easily avoided when one considers the other fifty-five pattern offerings in toy table sets, each of which contains a butter, sugar, creamer and spoon holder.

With more than twenty American and European beverage sets, only Westmoreland's Little Jo (Arched Panels) water set has been reissued in many colors. So far old sets have turned up in crystal, light pink, light green and rich amber. Some collectors claim cobalt to be old as well, but since it was also reproduced in cobalt, it is not as safe for the purist to buy as the other shades.

Out of eleven American punch set patterns, Inverted Strawberry, marked with an "M" for Mosser, has been reissued. Flattened Diamond also has many colors in its new punch set lineup. The company reproducing Buzz Star (Whirligig) has used the wrong punch bowl mould to produce a so-called toy punch set. The new bowls are 5⅞" tall, while the old punch bowl measures 4¼" in height and 4⅝" across. This #15101 pattern was originally a product of the United States Glass Company and was produced only in crystal.

Lacy Daisy is the only berry set to be remade. It was also called Crystal Jewel in the original ads found in early Butler Brothers Catalogues. This charming dessert set was reissued by Westmoreland.

If you do not want any new glass toy sets as part of your collection, then these are the patterns to avoid: Little Jo water set, Hawaiian Lei table set, Inverted Strawberry punch set, Lamb table set, Flattened Diamond table and punch sets, Tappan table set, Buzz Star (Whirligig) punch set, Lacy Daisy berry set and the Chimo creamer and spooner. To date, the rest are safe and still charming in their old age.

Figure Symbols

A	Akro Agate
B	Berry, Dessert, Fish sets
C	Candlesticks
CH	Chamber sets
CK	Carnival Kittens
COND	Condiment sets
CS	Castor sets
CUP	Cups and Saucers
D	Decanter sets
DE	Depression Era
E	Epergnes
L	Lemonade or water sets
LH	Lechler Heirlooms
LU	Lusters
M	Miscellaneous
M	Mugs
P	Punch sets
PL	Plates
S	Stein sets
SA	Sandwich miniatures
SO	Sowerby
TEA	Tea sets
TM	Tom Mosser
TS	Table sets
TU	Tumble Ups

INDEX

†Indicates an item is shown in color and black and white.
*Indicates an item has been reproduced.

UNIQUE TO AMERICAN TOY GLASS PATTERNS

There are only two patterns in the toy glass field which have all four units of pleasure: table set, berry set, lemonade or water set, and punch set. The two patterns which carry the complete range are Oval Star and Nursery Rhyme.

The Wabash series produced by Federal Glass Company in Columbus, Ohio, offers an unusual combination of toy glass for today's collectors. There is a five-to-seven-piece fish set, using the same moulds as the ABC ice cream set, a four-piece vegetable serving set, a four-piece table set with an additional butter dish, and a five-to-seven-piece punch set. There is also an elusive five-to-seven-piece grape stein set included in this wonderful series.

Other patterns have the following units: Colonial Flute has three units, but lacks a table set; Rex or Fancy Cut has three sets, but lacks a berry set; Pattee Cross has all but a table set; Wheat Sheaf offers a wine set, punch set and berry set, but does not present a table setting; Inverted Strawberry lacks a table and a water set; Wild Rose has a punch and a table set only, as does Buzz Star and Thumbelina or Flattened Diamond; The Michigan pattern has a water set, a table set and a stein unit; Chateau No. 714 has a punch set and a newly assembled table set.

Patterns with only table sets are: Acorn, Amazon, Austrian, Bead and Scroll, Beaded Swirl, Braided Belt, Large Block, Bucket, Button Arches, Button Panel, Cambridge Colonial, Cambridge Fernland, Chimo, Buzz Star, Sweetheart, Clambroth Scenery, Clear and Diamond Panels, Buzz Saw, Cloud Band, Dewdrop or Dot, Euclid or Rexford, Fine Cut Star and Fan; Hawaiian Lei, Heisey's Sawtooth Band, Hobnail/Thumbprint Base, Horizontal Threads, Lamb, Menagerie, Northwood Hobnail, Pennsylvania, Pert, Plain Pattern #13 or Double Ribbon Bar, Pointed Jewel, Tappan, Sawtooth, Standing Lamb, Stippled Dewdrop and Raindrop, Stippled Vine and Beads, Style or Arrowhead-In-Oval, Sultan, Sunbeam or Twin Snowshoes, Two Band, Twist, and Rooster.

There are table set patterns which have matching mugs, cup and saucer combinations and plates: Doyle #500 has a table set with a tray and mugs to match; Drum has a table set and mugs; Grape Vine and Ovals comes in a table set and mugs; Liberty Bell has a table set and mug; Lion has a table set, a cup and saucer; Stippled Diamond has a table set and mug; Wee Branches has a cup, saucer, plate and mug to match its table set.

Other pattern combinations include Baby Thumbprint which has two compotes, one covered and one flare-top uncovered, two cake plates and a butter dish; Dutch Boudoir has a bedroom set with a tray, two pomades, a candlestick or two, pitcher, bowl, slop jar, covered potty; D & M #42 has a table set with a honey jug and also a rose bowl in miniature; the Monk stein set has no other counterparts; Galloway, Portland, Banded Portland, Ruffled and Tankard Enamels, Cambridge No. 1, Hobbs, Little Jo, Petite and Square Hobnail, Stiegel, Optic and Mary Gregory are single unit lemonade or water sets; Fine Cut, Lacy Daisy, Baby Flute, Bullseye and Fan No. 15090 have only berry sets to their names.

The Rex pattern provides three sets special to a toy glass collection.

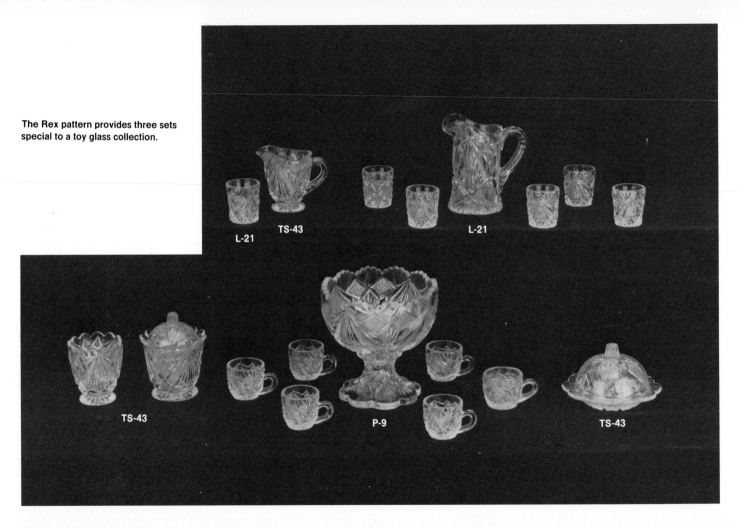

L-21   TS-43   L-21

TS-43   P-9   TS-43

Oval Star 300 is one of two patterns which carries all
four units typical of toy glass.

B-4

P-7

L-15

L-15

TS-39

The Wabash series by Federal Glass Co. offers an unusual combination-
selection of toy glass.

TS-55   TS-55   TS-55   TS-55   TS-55   S-1

TS-55A   TS-55A

        TS-55A   TS-55A   P-11

TYPICAL TOY GLASS ADS

15101 4-Piece Toy Table Set, $1.64 per doz.

15101 Toy Cream
38c per doz.

15101 Toy Sugar
50c per doz.

15101 Toy Butter
46c per doz.

15101 Toy Spoon
30c per doz.

15101 4-Piece Toy Set, Gold Decorated, $4.50 per doz.

15112 Toy Berry Set, 7 Pieces
Packed one set in pasteboard box, $1.60 per doz.
Gold Decorated, $4.70 per doz.

15101 Toy Punch Set, 7 Pieces
$3.00 per doz.
Packed one set in pasteboard box
Gold Decorated, $6.60 per doz.

15112 Toy Water Set, 7 Pieces
$2.50 per doz.
Packed one set in pasteboard box
Gold Decorated, $5.70 per doz

15090 Toy Dessert Set, 7 Pieces
One set in pasteboard box $1.60 per doz.

GILLINDER & SONS, Inc., PHILADELPHIA, PA.,

Manufacture a full line of

OPAL DECORATED NOVELTIES.

SEND

FOR

SAMPLES.

No. 4. Candlestick. Decorated.

No. 1. Smoking Set. Decorated. One set in a box.

Spoon Butter Sugar Cream

TOY SETS

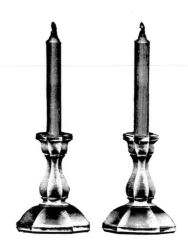

Two Candlesticks and three Candles packed complete in pasteboard box constitutes set.

Packs 2 dozen Sets to barrel

BEVERAGE SETS

Figure L-4
European
Enamel

Figure D-1
Rope of Sapphire

Figure D-2
French
Travel

Figure D-3
Tiny Tot Keg

Figure L-5
European Enamel
on tray

Figure D-4
Gold and Clear

Figure D-5
Enameled/Dotted
Flowers

Figure D-6
Whisk-shaped
Enameled Flowers

1

Figure D-7
Threaded

Figure D-8
Enameled Leaf and Vine

Figure D-9
Mirror and Fan

Figure D-10
Contemporary Frosted

Figure D-11
Sandwich (type)

Figure D-12
Johannesburg Frosted

Figure D-13
Silver Overlay

Figure PL-44
Twin

Figure PL-43
Twin

Figure L-15
Oval Star,
Crystal No. 300

3

Figure L-8
Hobbs

Figure PL-54
Baby Thumbprint

Figure L-2
Enameled
Ruffled

Figure B-3
Cambridge
Inverted
Strawberry

5

Figure L-7
Galloway

Figure L-20
Portland

Figure L-7
Galloway

L-10

Figure L-10
Little Jo,
Arched Panels

L-10

6

Figure L-2
Enameled
Ruffled

Figure L-3
Tankard
(style)

Figure L-2

Figure L-3

Figure L-3

Figure L-3

7

Figure P-6
Nursery Rhyme

8

Figure P-6
Nursery Rhyme

Figure TS-38
Nursery Rhyme

P-6

P-6

Figure B-2
Nursery
Rhyme

L-13
Nursery
Rhyme

9

Figure P-12
Wild Rose

Figure TS-59
Wild Rose

Figure P-12
Wild Rose

Figure S-3
Monk

Figure C-35
Wild Rose

Figure S-3
Monk

**Figure TEA-1
Ruby with Enamel**

**Figure L-1
Cobalt with Thistles**

**Figure L-6
Moser**

**Figure L-11
Mary Gregory**

11

Figure TU-1

Figure TU-2

Figure TU-3

Figure TU-4

Figure TU-5

Figure TU-6

Figure TU-7

Figure TU-8

Figure TU-9

Figure TU-10

Figure TU-11

Figure TU-12

Figure TU-13

Figure TU-14

Figure TU-15

Figure TU-16

Figure TU-17

Figure TU-18

Figure TU-19

Figure TU-20

12

Figure TU-27

Figure TU-28

Figure TU-29

Figure TU-30

Figure TU-31

Figure TU-32

Figure TU-33

Figure TU-34

Figure TU-35

Figure TU-36

Figure TU-37

Figure TU-38

Figure TU-39

Figure TU-40

Figure TU-41A

Figure TU-41

Figure TU-42

Figure TU-43

Figure TU-44

Figure TU-45

13

MISCELLANEOUS

Figure S-2
Michigan

Figure PL-52
Baby Thumbprint

Figure S-2
Michigan

Figure
E-1

Figure PL-68

Figure PL-67

Figure M-16

Figure D-14
Clear Swirl

Figure D-15
Enameled Dot
and Flower

Figure D-16
Dimpled

†Figure TEA-3
Clear with
Enamel

MISCELLANEOUS

Figure TU-17
Moser

Figure TEA-2
Beaded Glass

Figure TU-21

Figure TU-22

Figure TU-23

Figure TU-24

Figure TU-25

**Figure
LU-7**

Figure M-6

**Figure
LU-7**

Figure TU-26

15

MISCELLANEOUS

Figure M-1

Figure M-1

Figure M-2

Figure M-4

Figure M-5

Figure M-5

Figure SO-7

Figure M-3

Figure M-7

Figure M-8

Figure M-9

Figure M-10

Figure M-11

Figure M-12

CANDLESTICKS

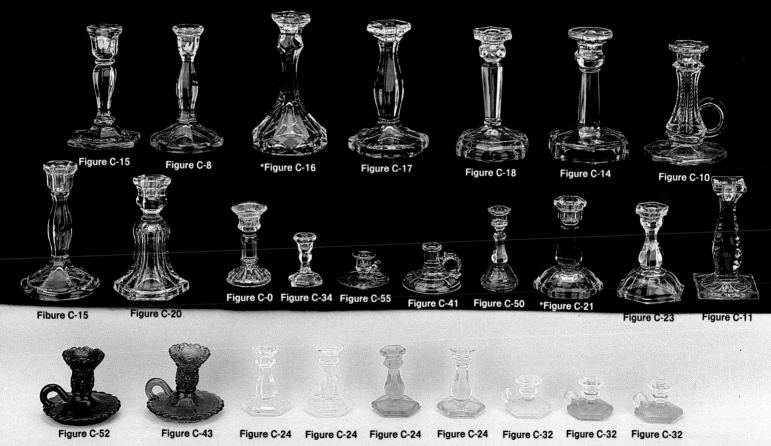

Figure C-15

Figure C-8

*Figure C-16

Figure C-17

Figure C-18

Figure C-14

Figure C-10

Fibure C-15

Figure C-20

Figure C-0   Figure C-34   Figure C-55

Figure C-41

Figure C-50

*Figure C-21

Figure C-23

Figure C-11

Figure C-52

Figure C-43

Figure C-24

Figure C-24

Figure C-24

Figure C-24

Figure C-32

Figure C-32

Figure C-32

17

Figure C-53

Figure C-36

*Figure C-54

Figure C-54

Figure C-54

Figure C-37

Figure C-35

*Figure C-26

*Figure C-25

*Figure C-26

Figure C-29

Figure C-26

Figure C-28

Figure C-42

Figure C-56

Figure C-57

Figure C-58

Figure C-34

Figure C-22

Figure C-59

Figure C-46

18

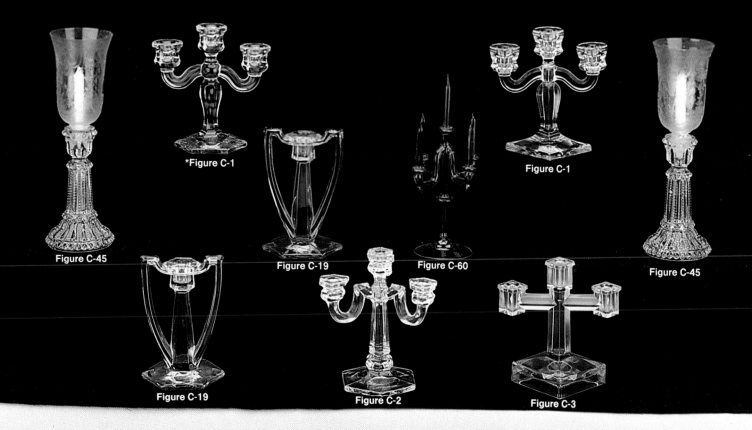

Figure C-45

*Figure C-1

Figure C-19

Figure C-60

Figure C-1

Figure C-45

Figure C-19

Figure C-2

Figure C-3

19

CARNIVAL KITTENS

Figure CK-1

Figure CK-2

Figure CK-3

Figure CK-4

Figure CK-5

Figure CK-2

Figure CK-3

Figure CK-6

Figure CK-7

20

CASTOR SETS

Figure CS-4   Figure CS-7   Figure CS-4   Figure CS-7   Figure CS-1   Figure CS-4

Figure CS-7   Figure CS-5   Figure CS-2   Figure CS-6   Figure CS-8   Figure CS-3   Figure CS-9

CASTOR SETS

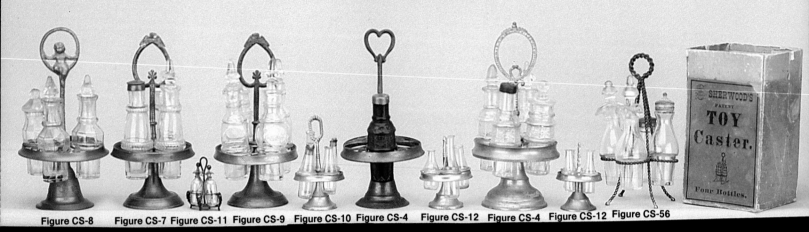

Figure CS-8 Figure CS-7 Figure CS-11 Figure CS-9 Figure CS-10 Figure CS-4 Figure CS-12 Figure CS-4 Figure CS-12 Figure CS-56

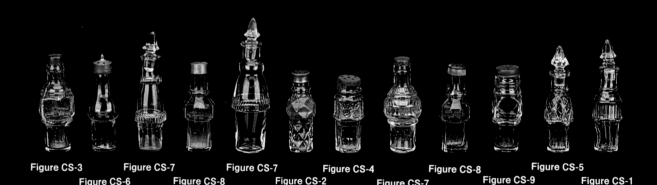

Figure CS-3 Figure CS-7 Figure CS-7 Figure CS-4 Figure CS-8 Figure CS-5

Figure CS-6 Figure CS-8 Figure CS-2 Figure CS-7 Figure CS-9 Figure CS-1

22

CHAMBER SETS

Figure CH-1
Dutch Boudoir

Figure CH-2

Figure CH-1
Dutch Boudoir

Figure CH-1
Dutch Boudoir

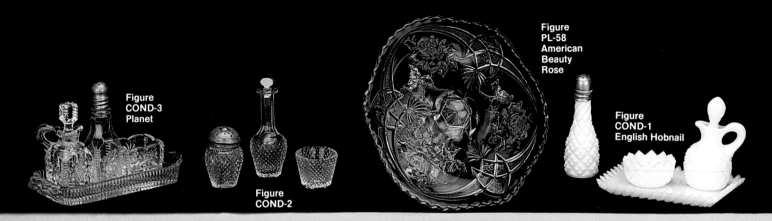

Figure
COND-3
Planet

Figure
COND-2

Figure
PL-58
American
Beauty
Rose

Figure
COND-1
English Hobnail

Figure
PL-64
Goofus

Figure
COND-4
Hickman

Figure
COND-1
English
Hobnail

Figure
PL-57
Ribbon
Candy

CUPS AND SAUCERS

Figure CUP-1

Figure CUP-2

Figure CUP-3

Figure CUP-4

Figure CUP-10

Figure CUP-11

Figure CUP-10

Figure CUP-5

Figure CUP-4

Figure CUP-6

Figure CUP-7

Figure CUP-8

Figure CUP-9

EPERGNES

**Figure
E-2**

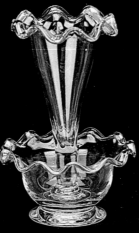

**Figure
E-3**

**Figure
E-4**

**Figure
E-5**

**Figure
E-6**

**Figure
E-7**

**Figure
E-8**

**Figure
E-9**

**Figure
E-18**

EPERGNES

Figure
E-10

Figure
E-11

Figure
E-12

Figure
E-13

Figure
E-14

Figure
E-15

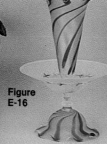

Figure M-15

Figure
E-16

Figure
E-17

27

LUSTERS

Figure LU-1

Figure LU-2

Figure LU-8

Figure LU-3

Figure LU-4

Figure LU-5

Figure LU-6

MUGS

†Figure M-1

†Figure M-2

Figure M-3

†Figure M-4

†Figure M-5

†Figure M-6

Figure M-7

Figure M-8

Figure M-9

Figure M-10

Figure M-11

†Figure M-12

†Figure M-13

†Figure M-14

Figure M-15

Figure M-16

†Figure M-17

Figure M-18

Figure M-19

Figure M-20

Figure M-21

Figure M-22

†Figure M-23

Figure M-24

Figure M-25

Figure M-26

Figure M-27

Figure M-27

Figure M-28

Figure M-29

29

Figure M-30

Figure M-31

Figure M-32

Figure M-33

Figure M-34

Figure M-35

Figure M-36

Figure M-37

Figure M-38

Figure M-39

Figure M-40

Figure M-41

Figure M-42

Figure M-43

Figure M-44

Figure M-45

Figure M-46

Figure M-47

Figure M-48

Figure M-49

Figure M-50

†Figure M-51

Figure M-52

Figure M-53

Figure M-76

Figure M-54

Figure M-55

Figure M-45

Figure M-56

Figure M-45

Figure M-57

30

Figure
M-58

Figure
M-59

Figure
M-60

Figure
M-61

Figure
M-62

Figure
M-63

†Figure
M-64

†Figure
M-65

†Figure
M-66

†Figure
M-67

†Figure
M-68

Figure
M-69

Figure
M-70

*†Figure
M-71

†Figure
M-72

†Figure
M-73

Figure
M-74

†Figure
M-75

SANDWICH MINIATURES

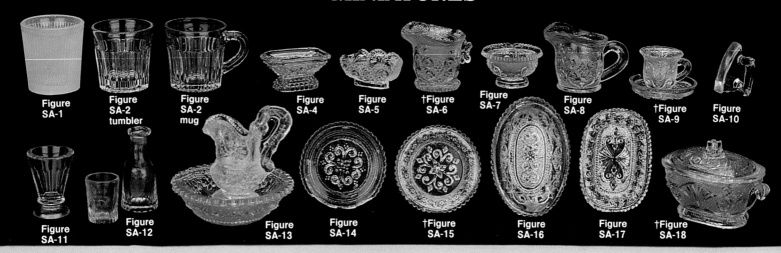

Figure
SA-1

Figure
SA-2
tumbler

Figure
SA-2
mug

Figure
SA-4

Figure
SA-5

†Figure
SA-6

Figure
SA-7

Figure
SA-8

†Figure
SA-9

Figure
SA-10

Figure
SA-11

Figure
SA-12

Figure
SA-13

Figure
SA-14

†Figure
SA-15

Figure
SA-16

Figure
SA-17

†Figure
SA-18

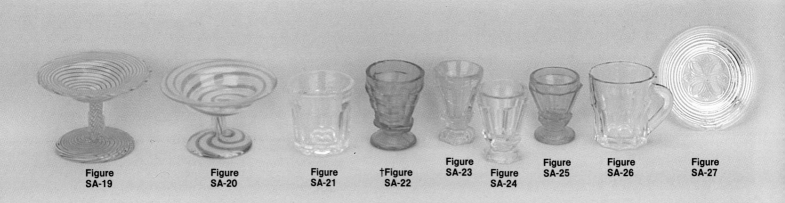

Figure
SA-19

Figure
SA-20

Figure
SA-21

†Figure
SA-22

Figure
SA-23

Figure
SA-24

Figure
SA-25

Figure
SA-26

Figure
SA-27

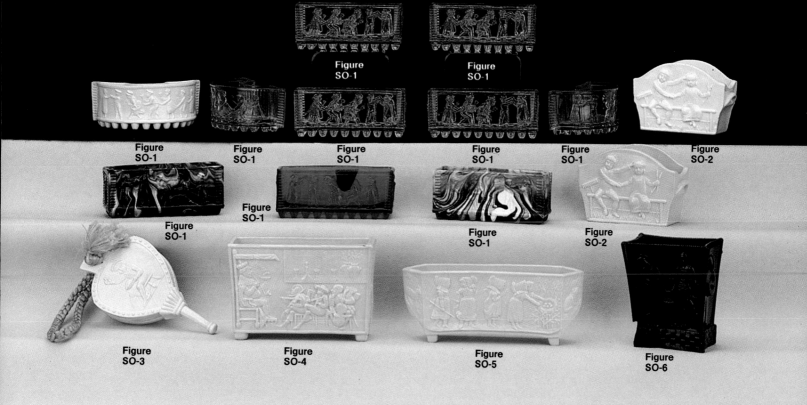

Figure
SO-1

Figure
SO-1

Figure
SO-1

Figure
SO-1

Figure
SO-1

Figure
SO-1

Figure
SO-1

Figure
SO-2

Figure
SO-1

Figure
SO-1

Figure
SO-1

Figure
SO-2

Figure
SO-3

Figure
SO-4

Figure
SO-5

Figure
SO-6

33

TABLE SETS

†Austrian

Figure TS-3

†Sultan

Figure TS-51

†Sultan
Figure TS-51

†Braided Belt
Figure TS-7

†Clambroth Scenery
Figure TS—17

Figure M-17

†Cloud Band
Figure TS-19

Figure TS-17

36

†(Large) Block

Figure TS-6

Figure TS-18

Figure TS-6

†Clear and Diamond Panels

Figure TS-18

37

†Heisey's Sawtooth Band
Figure TS-28

†Button Panel D and M #44
Figure TS-9

†Button Arches
Figure TS-60

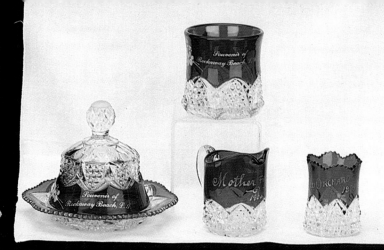

†*Lamb
Figure TS-31

Cambridge Contributions
Buzz Saw
Figure TS-10

Figure LO
No. 1

Fernland
Figure TS-13

Colonial
Figure TS-12

40

†Dewdrop, Dot
Figure TS-21

†Northwood Hobnail
Figure TS-37

Figure TS-21

†Hobnail with Thumbprint base
Figure TS-29

Figure TS-29

41

†Doyle #500
Figure TS-22

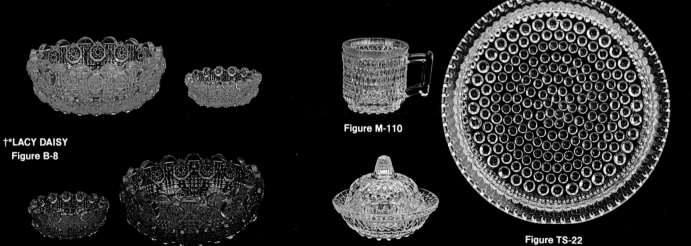

†*LACY DAISY
Figure B-8

Figure M-110

Figure TS-22

43

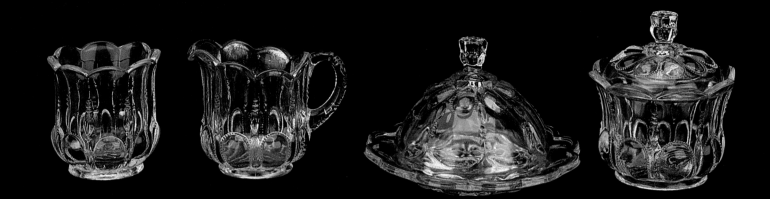

†Sultan
Figure TS-51

†Michigan
Figure TS-36

†Twist
Figure TS-56

†Pennsylvania No. 15048
Figure TS-40

†Clear and Diamond Panels
Figure TS-18

†Twist
Figure TS-56

45

†Pennsylvania No. 15048
Figure TS-40

Figure TS-40

†Twist
Figure TS-56

†Twist
Figure TS-56

†Stippled Raindrop
and Dewdrop
Figure TS-48

Figure TS-48

†Stippled Diamond
Figure TS-47

47

†Plain Pattern #13, Frosted Ribbon Double Bar
Figure TS-42

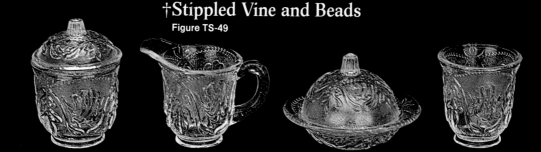

50

Figure P-10

Figure TS-54

Figure M-18

51

New toy glass
by Tom Mosser

Figure TM-1

Figure TM-2

Figure TM-2

Figure TM-3

Figure TM-4

Figure TM-4

Figure TM-5

Figure TM-8

Figure TM-9

Figure TM-9

Figure TM-11

Figure TM-12

Figure TM-13

Figure TM-13

Figure TM-14

Figure TM-13

Figure TM-13

New toy glass
by Tom Mosser

Figure TM-18

Figure TM-19

Figure TM-22

Figure TM-16

Figure TM-17

Figure TM-20

Figure TM-21

Figure TM-23

Figure TM-24

Figure TM-25

Figure TM-28

Figure TM-26

Figure TM-26

Figure TM-27

Figure TM-29

Figure TM-30

Figure TM-32

Figure TM-31

Figure TM-33

Figure TM-35

Figure TM-36

Figure TM-38

Figure TM-40

Figure TM-34

Figure TM-36

Figure TM-37

Figure TM-39

Figure TM-41

53

Contemporary
Toy
Glass

New L-10 New L-10 New L-10 New TS-31 New TS-31 New TS-31 Wetzel 1 Wetzel 2

New P-10 New P-10 New P-10 New P-10

New C-1 New B-1 New B-1 New C-1 New B-1 New B-1 New C-1

54

Lechler
Heirlooms of Tomorrow

New LH-1

New LH-2

New LH-3

New LH-4

New LH-5

New LH-6

New LH-7

55

Figure LH-8

Figure LH-9

Figure LH-10

Figure LH-11

Figure LH-12

Figure LH-13

Figure LH-14

Figure LH-15

Figure LH-16

Akro Agate

Figure A-1 Figure A-1 Figure A-2 Figure A- Figure A-1 Figure A-3 Figure A-4 Figure A-5 Figure A-0

Figure A-6 Figure A-7 Figure A-8 Figure A-9 Figure A-10 Figure A-10 Figure A-11 Figure A-12 Figure AA-12

Figure A-13 Figure A-14 Figure A-15 Figure A-16 Figure A-17 Figure A-18 Figure A-19 Figure A-20 Figure A-21 Figure A-22

Figure A-23 Figure A-24 Figure A-25 Figure A-26 Figure A-27 Figure A-28

57

Akro Agate

Figure A-38

Figure A-36

Figure A-44

Figure A-45

Figure A-37

Figure A-39

Figure A-40

Figure A-41

Figure A-42

Figure A-43

Figure A-46

Figure A-47

Figure A-48

Figure A-49

Figure A-50

Figure A-51

Figure A-52

Figure A-53

Figure A-54

Figure A-55

Figure A-56

Figure A-57

Figure A-58

Figure A-59

Figure A-60

Figure A-61

Figure A-64

Figure A-67

Figure A-70

Figure A-73

Figure A-62

Figure A-63

Figure A-65

Figure A-66

Figure A-68

Figure A-69

Figure A-71

Figure A-72

Figure A-74

Figure A-75

58

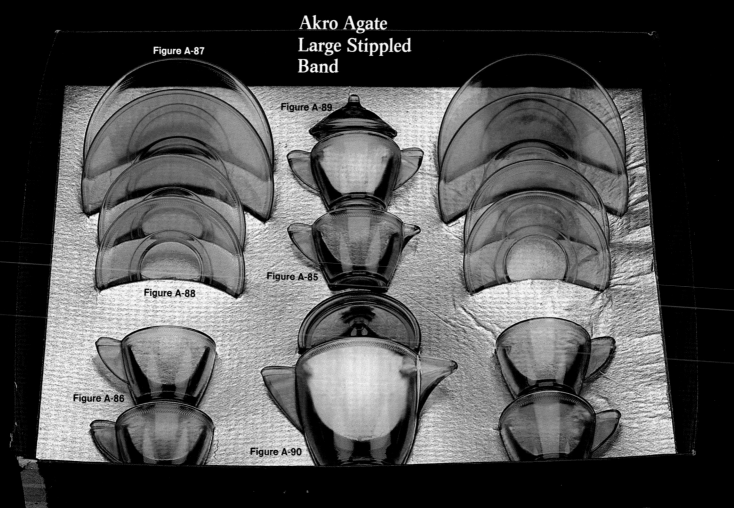

Figure A-87

Figure A-89

Figure A-88

Figure A-85

Figure A-86

Figure A-90

Marbelized, Small
Interior Panel

Akro Agate

Luster, Small
Interior Panel

Figure A-93

Figure A-94

Figure A-92

Figure A-95

Figure A-98

Figure A-99

Figure A-97

Figure A-100

Figure A-102

PLAY-TIME

AKRO WATER SET

PLAY AA TIME

Figure A-103

Raised Daisy

Figure A-108   Figure A-106

Figure A-109

Figure A-107   Figure A-105
cup

AMERICAN MAID TEA SET

THE LITTLE
AMERICAN MAID
TEA SET

Akro Agate

PLAY-TIME
GLASS WATER SET

PLAY-TIME
GLASS DISHES

Figure A-117

Figure A-116

Figure A-113

Figure A-112

Figure A-115

Figure A-118

62

Akro Agate

Figure A-120

Figure A-121

Figure A-122

Figure A-123

Figure A-124

Figure A-125

Figure A-126

Figure A-127

Figure A-128

Figure A-129

Figure A-130

Figure A-131

Figure A-132

Figure A-133

Figure A-134

Figure A-135

Figure A-136

Figure A-137

Figure A-138

Figure A-139

Figure A-140

Figure A-141

Figure A-142

Figure A-143

gure A-144

Figure A-145

Figure A-146

Figure A-147

Figure A-148

Figure A-149

Figure A-150

Figure A-151

Figure A-152

Figure A-153

Figure A-154

Figure A-155

63

Moderntone

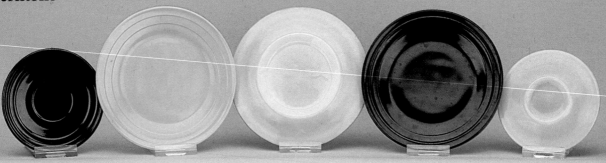

Figure DE-1   Figure DE-2

AKRO Agate

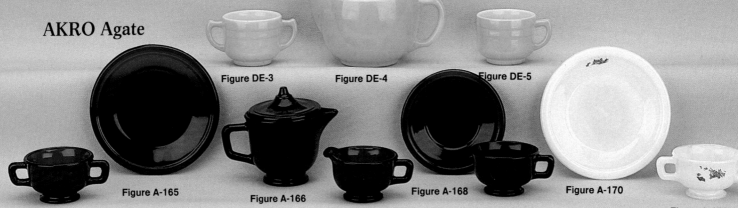

Figure DE-3   Figure DE-4   Figure DE-5

Figure A-164   Figure A-165   Figure A-166   Figure A-167   Figure A-168   Figure A-169   Figure A-170   Figure A-171

In this book, TOY GLASS, Bob Rogers accepted the task of amassing Akro sets, taking examples from his own collection and those of Joan Wood, Dick Walters, and Helen Haskell. Bob, in his quiet, methodical way gave me details which I gladly share with you.

There is much to know about this particular grouping, and those who have participated in making this section work find me deeply grateful.

AKRO AGATE

by
Mr. Bob Rogers

The Akro Agate Company was established in 1911 in Akron, Ohio, but moved to Clarksburg, West Virginia, in 1914. West Virginia offered cheap natural gas, as well as fine sand. These items were necessary for quality glassmaking. The new company's main product was marbles, but in 1935 children's dishes were started as a side line.

The children's dishes were introduced in transparent glass in topaz, green, and blue with the topaz being the oldest. Transparent red pieces have been discovered in the Miss America pattern as well as the Stippled Band pattern.

Jade and pink luster were the first opaques produced in 1935 until Akro began to mix colors in 1937. They continued to be successful through their peak years of 1942 and 1943 until they ceased to produce dishes in 1948. The company stopped operations and closed its doors in 1951.

Throughout the history of the company, Akro experimented with a variety of colors. Marbleized colors in orange/white, green/white, blue/white, and red/white are all examples of the dual colors. Lemonade and oxblood remains as the champion of glassmaking expertise because of the intricate process involved in keeping the red from bleeding into the lemon color.

The Miss America pattern is probably the rarest of all the examples of Akro children's dishes. Examples of this have been found in opaque white, opaque white with decals, orange with white, marbleized, transparent forest green, and transparent red.

Most of the sets of Akro Agate in this publication belong to Bob Rogers with additional loans from Dick Walters and Joan Wood. The Modern Tone set belongs to Helen Haskell. The Houze items shown here are from the Largent collection.

Listings appear top row, left to right as shown on color pages.

These sets are priced for seventeen-piece sets, in the small size, unless pictured. The large sets are priced as twenty-one piece sets, unless pictured.

Sets come in boxes of eight, ten, fourteen, sixteen, twenty-one and twenty-eight piece sets.

Figure A-1 tumbler, 2″ Stacked Disc and Interior Panel, transparent blue; $9-$10.

Figure A-2 pitcher, 2⅞″ Stacked Disc and Interior Panel, transparent blue; $18-$20.

Figure A-3 tea pot/lid, 3¾″ large Stacked Disc and Interior Panel, transparent blue; $40-$45.

Figure A-4 cereal, 3⅜″ large Stacked Disc and Interior Panel, transparent blue; $20-$24.

Figure A-5 tumbler, 2″ Stacked Disc and Interior Panel, Transparent green; $9-$10.

Figure A-0 pitcher, 2⅞″ Stacked Disc and Interior Panel, transparent green; $10-$12.

Figure A-6 creamer, 1⅜″, large Stacked Disc and Interior Panel, transparent blue; $20-$24.

Figure A-7 sugar/lid, 1⅞″ large Stacked Disc and Interior Panel, transparent blue; $35-$40.

Figure A-8 cup, 1⅜″ large Stacked Disc and Interior Panel, transparent blue; $18-$20.

Figure A-9 saucer, 3⅛″ large Stacked Disc and Interior Panel, transparent blue; $6-$8.

Figure A-10 sugar, also creamer, 1¼″ small Stacked Disc and Interior Panel, transparent blue; $20-$25.

Figure A-11 tea pot/lid, 3⅜″ small Stacked Disc and Interior Panel, transparent blue; $30-$35.

Figure A-12 cup, 1¼″ small Stacked Disc and Interior Panel, transparent blue; $18-$20.

Figure AA-12 saucer, 2¾″, small Stacked Disc and Interior Panel, transparent blue; $6-$8.

Figure A-13 cup, 1¼″ small Stacked Disc with Interior Panel, blue and white marbleized; $25-$30.

Figure A-14 saucer, 2⅜″ small Stacked Disc Interior Panel, blue and white marbleized; $10-$12.

Figure A-15 creamer, 1¼″ small Interior Panel; $25-$28.

Figure A-16 sugar, 1¼″; $25-$28.

Figure A-17 cup, 1¼″ small Stacked Disc and Interior Panel, yellow with orange opaque; $10-$15.

Figure A-18 cup 1⅜″ large Stacked Disc with Interior Panel, yellow with orange opaque; $18-$20.

Figure A-19 saucer, 3⅛″ large Stacked Disc and Interior Panel, yellow opaque; $4-$6.

Figure A-20 saucer, 2⅜″ small Interior Panel, jade luster; $3-$4.

Figure A-21 saucer, 2⅜″ small Interior Panel; $5-$8.

Figure A-22 plate, 3¾″ small Interior Panel, yellow opaque; $8-$10.

Figure A-23 sugar, 1¼″ small Stacked Disc and Interior Panel, blue opaque; $6-$8.

Figure A-24 tea pot/lid, 3⅜″ small Stacked Disc and Interior Panel, blue opaque; $15-$18.

Figure A-25 tea pot/lid, 3¾″ large Stacked Disc and Interior Panel, cobalt opaque; $35-$40.

Figure A-26 creamer 1⅜″ large Stacked Disc and Interior Panel, cobalt opaque; $12-$15.

Figure A-27 sugar/lid, 1⅞″ large Stacked Disc and Interior Panel, cobalt opaque; $20-$25.

Figure A-28 tea pot/lid, 3⅜″ small Stacked Disc Interior Panel, blue/white marbleized; $45-$50.

Figure A-29 Stacked Disc Interior Panel, transparent blue water set; collection: Rogers; $72-$80.

Figure A-30 Stacked Disc Interior Panel transparent green water set; collection: Rogers; $64-$72.

Figure A-31 Large Stacked Disc Interior Panel, transparent blue set; collection: Rogers; $311-$366.

Figure A-32 Small Stacked Disc Interior Panel, transparent blue set; collection: Rogers; $206-$245.

Figure A-33 Small Stacked Disc Interior Panel, blue/white marbleized set; collection: Rogers; $293-$344.

Figure A-34 Small Stacked Disc Interior Panel, yellow/ orange opaque set; collection: Rogers; $107-$146.

Figure A-35 Small Interior Panel, jade luster set; collection: Rogers; $170-$200.

Figure A-36 cup, 1¹³/₁₆″ Raised Daisy, green opaque; $10-$12.

Figure A-37 saucer, 2½″ Raised Daisy, yellow opaque; $7-$8.

Figure A-38 plate, 3″ Raised Daisy, blue opaque; $8-$10.

Figure A-39 tea pot, 2⅜″ Raised Daisy, no daisy, opaque; $18-$20.

Figure A-40 tea pot, 2⅜″, Raised Daisy, with daisy, opaque; $18-$20.

Figure A-41 tea pot, 2⅜″ Raised Daisy, no daisy opaque with decal; $20-$25.

Figure A-42 sugar/lid, 2⅞″ Houze Company, yellow; $25-$30.

Figure A-43 creamer, 1¾″, Houze Company, green; $15-$20.

Figure A-44 plate, 4″ Houze Company, blue; $10-$15.

Figure A-45 cup, 1¼″ Houze Company, blue; $20-$25.

Figure A-46 saucer, 3¼″, Houze Company, blue; $8-$10. set of Houze, $240-$300.

Figure A-47 tea pot/lid, 3⅜″, small Octagonal, blue opaque, open handle; $12-$16.

Figure A-48 tea pot/lid, 3⅜″, large Octagonal, blue opaque, open handle; $18-$20.

Figure A-49 pitcher, 2⅞″, Stacked Disc, blue opaque; $7-$8.

Figure A-50 tumbler, 2″ Stacked Disc, yellow opaque; $4-$5.

Figure A-51 tumbler, 1¾″, Stippled Band; Interior Panel, transparent topaz; $7-$8.

Figure A-52 tumbler, 1¾″, Stippled Band, transparent topaz; $5-$6.

Figure A-53 pitcher, 2⅞″, Stippled Band, transparent topaz; $8-$10.

Figure A-54 sugar, 1¼″, small Octagonal, blue opaque, open handle; $12-$14.

Figure A-55 creamer, 1¼″, small Octagonal, blue opaque, open handle; $12-$14.

Figure A-56 sugar/lid, large Octagonal, blue opaque, open handle; $8-$10.

Figure A-57 creamer, 1½″, large Octagonal, blue opaque, open handle; $8-$10.

Figure A-58 tea pot, 3⅜″, small Stippled Band, transparent topaz; $12-$14.

Figure A-59 cereal, 3⅜″ large Concentric Ring, blue opaque; $16-$18.

Figure A-60 cup, 1¼″ small Concentric Ring, transparent blue; $25-$28.

Figure A-61 plate, 3⅜″ large Octagonal, lime opaque; $3-$4.

Figure A-62 cup, 1¼″ large Octagonal, pumpkin opaque, open handle; $8-$10.

Figure A-63 saucer, 2¾″ large Octagonal, yellow opaque, $2-$3.

Figure A-64 plate, 3¼″ small Concentric Ring, lavender opaque; $12-$16.

Figure A-65 cup, 1¼″ small Concentric Ring, lavender opaque; $20-$24.

Figure A-66 saucer, 2¾″, small Concentric Ring, pink opaque; $4-$5.

Figure A-67 plate, 3⅜″, small Octagonal, green opaque; $3-$4.

Figure A-68 cup, 1¼″ small Octagonal, closed handle; no serving pieces have been located to date for small closed handled Octagonal, pumpkin opaque; $20-$25.

Figure A-69 saucer, 2¾″, small Octagonal, yellow opaque; $2-$3.

Figure A-70 plate, 3¼″ small Stippled Band, transparent topaz; $4-$6.

Figure A-71 cup, 1¼″ small Stippled Band, transparent topaz; $6-$8.

Figure A-72 saucer, 2¾″, small Stippled Band, transparent topaz; $2-$4.

Figure A-73 plate, 4¼″, large Concentric Ring, lime opaque; $6-$8.

Figure A-74 cup, 1⅜″, large Concentric Ring, pumpkin opaque; $15-$16.

Figure A-75 saucer, 3⅛″, large Concentric Ring, yellow opaque; $5-$6.

Raised Daisy, collection: Rogers; $188-$200.

Figure A-77 small Octagonal open handled set, collection: Rogers; $96-$120.

Stacked Disc water set, collection: Rogers; $31-$38.

Stippled Band Interior Panel transparent topaz water set, collection: Rogers; $54-$63.

Large Concentric Ring opaque set, collection: Rogers; $235-$275.

Large Octagonal open handled set, collection: Walters; $110-$140.

Stippled Band transparent topaz water set, collection: Rogers; $38-$46.

Small Concentric Ring, transparent blue, collection: Rogers; $250-$297.

Small Concentric Ring opaque, collection: Walters; $107-$134.

Boxed set of large Stippled Band, transparent azure:

Figure A-85 creamer, 1½″ $35-$40.

Figure A-86 cup, 1½″ $20-$25.

Figure A-87 plate, 4¼″ $12-$15.

Figure A-88 saucer, 3¼″ $10-$12.

Figure A-89 sugar/lid, $40-$45.

Figure A-90 tea pot/lid, 3¾″ $50-$55.

Collection: Rogers

Boxed set: $293-$348.

Boxed set of red and whtie marbleized small Interior Panel:

Figure A-92 cup, 1¼″ $20-$25.

Figure A-93 plate, 3¾″ $9-$10.

Figure A-94 saucer, 2⅜″ $6-$8.

Figure A-95 tea pot/lid, 3⅜″ $30-$35.

Collection: Rogers

Figure A-96 boxed set: $100-$120.

Boxed set, pink luster, small Interior Panel:

Figure A-97 cup, 1¼″ $7-$10.

Figure A-98 plate, 3¾″ $4-$5.

Figure A-99 saucer, 2⅜″ $4-$5.

Figure A-100 tea pot/lid, 3⅜″ $18-$20.

Collection: Rogers

Figure A-101 boxed set: $48-$60.

Raised Daisy water set; blue tumblers without daisies are difficult to locate:

Figure A-102 pitcher, 2⅜″ $18-$20.

Figure A-103 tumbler, 2″ $15-$18.

Collection: Rogers

Figure A-104 set: $78-$90.

Boxed set, large Octagonal, closed handle, found in opaques and Lemonade and oxblood:

Figure A-105 cup, 1½″ $6-$8.

Figure A-106 plate, 4¼″ $3-$4.

Figure A-107 sugar/lid, $6-$8.

Figure A-108 creamer, 1½″ $5-$6.

Figure A-109 tea pot/lid, $8-$10.

Figure A-110 cereal, 3⅜″ (not pictured), $6-$8.

Collection: Rogers

Figure A-111 boxed set with 17 pieces: $55-$72.

Boxed set, Small Octagonal water set:

Figure A-112 pitcher, 2⅞″ $10-$12.

Figure A-113 tumbler, 2″ $4-$6.

Collection: Rogers

Figure A-114 boxed set: $34-$48.

Boxed set, small Interior Panel, jade luster:

Figure A-115 cup, 1¼" $6-$8.

Figure A-116 saucer, 2⅜" $3-$4.

Figure A-117 plate, 3¾" $3-$4.

Figure A-118 tea pot/lid, 3⅜" $8-$12.

Collection: Rogers

Figure A-119 boxed set: $32-$44.

Figure A-120 creamer, 1⅜"; large Interior Panel; green/white marbleized; $16-$18.

Figure A-121 sugar/lid, 1⅞" large Interior Panel, green/white marbleized; $22-$25.

Figure A-122 creamer, 1⅜", large Interior Panel; Lemonade and Oxblood; $25-$30.

Figure A-123 sugar/lid, large Interior Panel; Lemonade and Oxblood; $30-$35.

Figure A-124 creamer, 1¼", small Interior Panel; blue/white marbleized; $22-$25.

Figure A-125 sugar, small Interior Panel, blue/white marbleized; $22-$25.

Figure A-126 tea pot/lid, 3⅜"; small Interior Panel; green/white marbleized; $25-$30.

Figure A-127 tea pot/lid, 3⅜", small Interior Panel; turquoise; $25-$30.

Figure A-128 tea pot/lid, 3¾", large Interior Panel; transparent topaz; $15-$20.

Figure A-129 tea pot/lid 3⅜", small Interior Panel; transparent topaz; $15-$20.

Figure A-130 sugar/lid, 1⅞"; large Interior Panel; transparent topaz; $15-$20.

Figure A-131 tea pot/lid, 3¾"; large Interior Panel; Lemonade and Oxblood; $45-$50.

Figure A-132 tea pot/lid, 3⅜", small Interior Panel; blue/white marbleized; $45-$50.

Figure A-133 cereal, 3⅜"; large Interior Panel; green/white marbleized; $18-$20.

Figure A-134 saucer, small Interior Panel; transparent topaz; $5-$6.

Figure A-135 cup, 1¼", small Interior Panel; transparent topaz; $10-$12.

Figure A-136 plate, 3¾", small Interior Panel; transparent topaz; $8-$10.

Figure A-137 saucer, 2⅜", small Interior Panel; blue/white marbleized; $8-$9.

Figure A-138 cup, 1¼", small Interior Panel; blue/white marbleized; $20-$25.

Figure A-139 plate, 3¾", small Interior Panel; blue/white marbleized; $10-$12.

Figure A-140 saucer, 2⅜"; small Interior Panel; green and white marbleized; $4-$5.

Figure A-141 cup, 1¼"; small Interior Panel; green/white marbleized; $6-$8.

Figure A-142 plate, 3¾"; small Interior Panel; green/white marbleized $6-$8.

Figure A-143 cereal, 3⅜"; large Interior Panel; Lemonade and Oxblood; $25-$30.

Figure A-144 saucer, 3⅛"/ large Interior Panel; transparent topaz, $6-$8.

Figure A-145 cup, 1⅜", large Interior Panel; transparent topaz; $10-$15.

Figure A-146 plate, 4¼"; large Interior Panel; transparent topaz; $8-$10.

Figure A-147 saucer, 3⅛"; large Interior Panel; green/white marbleized; $8-$10.

Figure A-148 cup, 1⅜"; large Interior Panel; green/white marbleized; $15-$18.

Figure A-149 plate, large Interior Panel; green/white marbleized; $10-$12.

Figure A-150 saucer, 3⅛"; large Interior Panel; pink luster; $4-$5.

Figure A-151 cup, 1⅜"; large Interior Panel; pink luster; $8-$10.

Figure A-152 plate, 4¼"; large Interior Panel; pink luster; $6-$8.

Figure A-153 saucer, 3⅛"; large Interior Panel; Lemonade and Oxblood; $8-$10.

Figure A-154 cup, 1⅜"; large Interior Panel; Lemonade and Oxblood; $25-$28.

Figure A-155 plate, 4¼"; large Interior Panel; Lemonade and Oxblood; $10-$12.

Large Interior Panel set; green/white marbleized; collection: Rogers; $274-$318.

Large Interior Panel set; Lemonade and Oxblood; collection: Rogers; $372-$435.

Small Interior Panel set; blue/white marbleized; collection: Walters; $228-$270.

Small Interior Panel set; green/white marbleized; collection: Rogers; $135-$166.

Small Interior Panel set; yellow or turquoise; collection: Rogers; $195-$246.

Small Interior Panel set; transparent topaz; collection: Rogers; $167-$202.

Large Interior Panel set; transparent topaz; collection: Rogers; $184-$247.

Large Interior Panel set; pink luster; collection: Rogers; $176-$215.

Miss America, very rare transparent red, solid white, orange with white marbleized, forest green, footed cups:

Figure A-164 sugar/lid, $62-$68.

Figure A-165 plate, $16-$20.

Figure A-166 tea pot/lid, $80-$88.

Figure A-167 creamer $42-$48.

Figure A-168 saucer, $12-$15.

Figure A-169 cup, $30-$35.

Figure A-170 plate, solid white/decals, $10-$14.

Figure A-171 sugar/lid, solid white/decals, $35-$40. collection: dark green, Woods

Set of dark green: $430-$485.

Set of white/decals: $270-$295.

Stacked Disc boxed water set

Figure A-174 pitcher, $7-$8.

Figure A-175 tumbler, $4-$5.

Figure A-176 boxed set, $31-$38.

Little Orphan Annie; made by Akro Agate for the H. Pressman Company

Figure A-177 creamer, 1½"; $25-$27.50.

Figure A-178 cup, 1½"; $15-$18.

Figure A-179 plate, 4¼"; $10-$12.50.

Figure A-180 saucer, 3¼"; $6-$7.50.

Figure A-181 sugar/lid, 1½"; $30-$32.50.

Figure A-182 tea pot, $37.50-$40.

Figure A-183 boxed set, $221-$258.

Stacked Disc boxed water set;
pitcher A-174, tumbler A-175

Little Orphan Annie boxed set, A-183; teapot, A-182; creamer, A-177; sugar, A-181; cup, A-178; saucer, A-180; plate, A-179.

Lemonade and Oxblood boxed set, A-192; creamer, A-186; saucer, A-189; teapot, A-191; sugar, A-190; cereal, A-185; plate, A-188.

Large Octagonal Lemonade and Oxblood

Figure A-185 cereal 3⅜"; $23-$28.

Figure A-186 creamer, 1½"; $23-$28.

Figure A-187 cup, 1½"; $22-$25.

Figure A-188 plate, 4¼"; $8-$10.

Figure A-189 saucer, 3⅜"; $7-$9.

Figure A-190 sugar/lid, $28-$32.

Figure A-191 tea pot/lid, 3½"; $40-$45.

Figure A-192 boxed set; $331-$393.

DEPRESSION ERA GLASS

Moderntone, Hazel Atlas Co., shown in pink and black, other color combinations: orange, gold, grey, turquoise; beige, turquoise, lemon, rose; green, wine, grey chartreuse; pastels: light pink, yellow, blue, green, pink.

Figure DE-1 saucer, 3⅞" $3.25-$3.75.

Figure DE-2 plate, 5¼" $3.50-$3.75.

Figure DE-3 sugar, 1¾" $4.50-$5.00.

Figure DE-4 tea pot/lid, 3½" $30-$35.

Figure DE-5 cup, 1¾" $4-$5.00.

Creamer, not shown, 1¾" $4.50-$5.00.

Collection: Haskell

Set: $82-$94.

74

DEPRESSION ERA WARE

Homespun, Jeannette Glass Company; between 1939 and 1940; pink, crystal; only true depression set to include a tea pot in the unit.

Figure DE-8 cup, clear, 1⅝" $16-$18.

Figure DE-9 cup, pink, $30-$35.

Figure DE-10 plate, clear, 4½" $6-$8.

Figure DE-11 plate, pink, $7-$10.

Figure DE-12 saucer, clear, 3¼" $3-$4.

Figure DE-13 saucer, pink, $5-$8.

Figure DE-14 tea pot/lid, 3¾" $50-$75.

Figure DE-15 boxed 14 piece set, pink, $200-$275; clear, $150-$200.

Betty Jane baking set: McKee Glass Co.; sets must be boxed to have value.

oval bake dish, 4¼" x 6⅜"

bowl, 3⅝"

bread pan, 3" x 4½"

covered casserole, 3⅛"

pie plate, 4½"

Figure DE-17 boxed set: $25-$40.

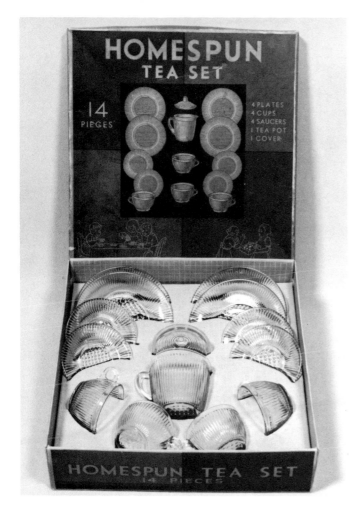

Betty Jane boxed baking set, DE-17.

Homespun boxed set, DE-15; teapot, DE-14; cup, DE-9; saucer, DE-13; plate, DE-11.

Sunny Suzy boxed baking set, DE-18.

Sunny Suzy glass baking set: Wolverine Supply Co. Pittsburgh, Pa., #261; Anchor Hocking; circa 1940s; sets must be boxed to have value.

2-handled baking dish, 10 oz.

custard cup, 5 oz.

casserole

Figure DE-18 boxed set, $25-$35.00.

Berry Sets

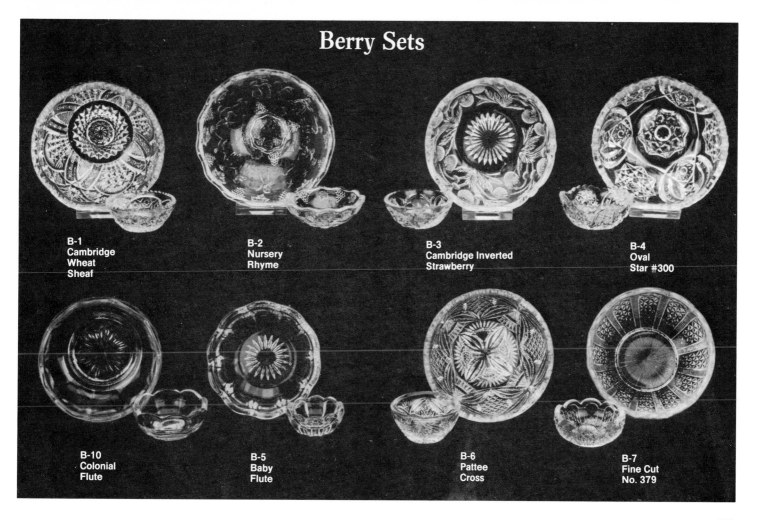

B-1
Cambridge
Wheat
Sheaf

B-2
Nursery
Rhyme

B-3
Cambridge Inverted
Strawberry

B-4
Oval
Star #300

B-10
Colonial
Flute

B-5
Baby
Flute

B-6
Pattee
Cross

B-7
Fine Cut
No. 379

BERRY AND DESSSERT SETS

BERRY, DESSERT and FISH SETS

One of the biggest thrills in the toy china realm is to discover a dessert set. They are very rare and cause an untold amount of panic and joy when there is one for sale.

The toy glass collecting field is blessed with several examples of quaint berry and dessert sets, some being more rare than others.

A berry set contains a main bowl which looks a bit like an adult sauce and indeed serves as such in some cases. The small bowl resembles a salt dip and many sets are completed by finding just what is needed in someone's salt dip collection.

A dessert set is another matter. They are more rare. For instance the ABC ice cream set has an oval platter and six small counterparts in the round. It was made in Columbus, Ohio, by the Federal Glass Company and many were left in the United States. The same mould was used for a different type of set which is certainly not a dessert unit. The mountain of ice cream was placed by a spot mould sporting a fish. Collectors believe the fish set was exported because very few collections have a complete seven piece fish set.

Prices vary for berry sets, some going for $75, such as the common Lacy Daisy in crystal. Add a little color to this same pattern and the set escalates to $300 or $400. You may view the amber and green berry set in the color section of this book. A blue set has just been discovered.

Counting the elusive berry set, shown below, in catalogue proof from the United States Glass Company, commonly known as Bull's Eye and Fan, there are ten berry sets to collect, one ice cream dessert set to find, and one fish set to wish for.

15090 Toy Dessert Set, 7 Pieces
One set in pasteboard box $1.60 per doz.

Figure B-1 CAMBRIDGE WHEAT SHEAF: five to seven piece punch set, five to seven piece berry set, five to seven piece decanter set; clear; all available; not reproduced.

main berry, 2¼" $50-$75.

small berry, 1" $7-$8.50.

set, $75-$150.

Collection: Lechler

Figure B-2 NURSERY RHYME: four piece table set, five to seven piece water set, five to seven piece punch set, five to seven piece berry set; clear; not reproduced.

main berry, 1⅜″ x 4½″ $100-$135.
small berry, 1¼″ x 2½″ $25-$35.
berry set, $225-$300.
Collection: Lechler

Figure B-3 CAMBRIDGE INVERTED STRAWBERRY: *five to seven piece punch set, five to seven piece berry set, clear only; berry set has not been reproduced; see cover for color picture.

main berry, 1⅝″ $75-$90.

small berry, ½″ $22-$25.

set, $200-$250.

Collection: Lechler

Figure B-4 OVAL STAR No. 300: Indiana Glass Company; four piece table set, five to seven piece punch set, berry set, water set; clear with or without gold; not reproduced.

main berry, 2″ $65-$85.

small berry, 1″ $10-$12.

set, $125-$175.

set with good gold, $150-$185.

collection: Lechler

No. 300 **Toy Berry Set**
(CRYSTAL)

One set packed complete in pasteboard box
Packs 2½ doz. Sets to barrel

Figure B-4
Oval Star, No. 300

Figure B-10 COLONIAL FLUTE: five to seven piece water set, five to seven piece punch set, five to seven piece berry

79

set; berry set in clear with or without gold trim; not reproduced.

main berry, $25-$35.

small berry, $6-$8.

berry set, $50-$75.

collection: Lechler

Figure B-5 BABY FLUTE: five to seven piece berry set; 20 point ray in base with ten fluted panels on main berry; 16 point rayed design in base of small berry; rare; not reproduced.

main berry, 1" x 3½" $80-$100.

small berry, ¾" x 1¾" $40-$50.

berry set, $175-$275.

Collection: Lechler

Figure B-6 PATTEE CROSS: five to seven piece water set, five to seven piece punch set, five to seven piece berry set; clear with or without gold; not reproduced.

main berry, 1¾" $35-$45.

small berry, 1" $12-$18.

berry set, $100-$125.

Collection: Lechler

Figure B-7 FINE CUT, No. 379: Co-Operative Flint Glass Company; five to seven piece berry set; clear; not reproduced.

main berry, 1¾" $65-$85.

small berry, ⅞" $8-$12.

berry set, $100-$125.

Collection: Lechler

Figure B-8†* LACY DAISY, Crystal Jewel: United States Glass Company; *five to seven piece berry set; old sets were produced in crystal, amber, blue and mint green; heavily reproduced.

main berry, clear, 1⅝" $30-$40.

main berry, color, $125-$150.

small berry, clear, 1" $5-$8.

small berry, color, $40-$60.

clear berry set, $60-$75.

color berry set, $350-$450.

Collection: Lechler

Figure B-9 ABC ICE CREAM SET: Wabash Series Federal Glass Company, Columbus, Ohio.

oval main platter, 5¾" x 4½", $150-$175.

small oval plate, 2¾" $50-$60.

set for six, $475-$525.

Collection: Lechler

Figure B-11 Same blank (except for) fish in the place of ice cream.

oval platter, $375-$400.

small round plate, $100-$125.

fish set for six, $800-$1000.

Collection: main platter, Lechler

Sundries

379—Toy Berry Set
5 piece Bulk, 12 doz. in bbl. Wt. 165 lbs.
5 piece boxed, 9 doz. in bbl., wt. 120 lbs.

Figure B-7
Fine Cut, No. 379
berry set ad

Figure B-6
Pattee Cross berry set ad.

15112 Toy Berry Set, 7 Pieces
Packed one set in pasteboard box, $1.60 per doz.
Gold Decorated, $4.70 per doz.

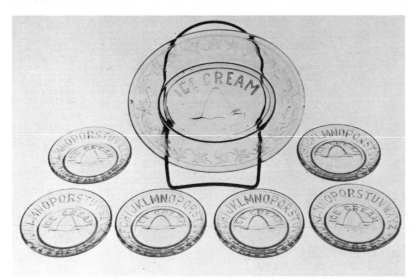

B-9 ABC ice cream

B-11 ABC fish

Fish Set

82

BEVERAGE SETS

Decanter Sets
Lemonade Sets
Punch Sets
Stein Sets
Tea Sets
Tumble Ups

You will find both American and European miniature beverage sets in this publication. Both hold important places of esteem in a collector's assemblage. The American sets have stable, no-nonsense hues with evident purpose. The European selections add color, gaiety and a range of interest which is unique to today's collections.

Because the early glass artists came from Europe bringing their traditions and ideas to their American glass houses, decanter sets, tumble ups and other vessels for liquid quickly became a part of the toy glass market. These items are included here because they are a part of toy glass history.

Only one American toy lemonade or water set has been reproduced to date. Little Jo (or Arched Panels) has received some color blows in the last few years. Originally this set seems to have been produced in crystal, old amber, light pink and light green. Some collectors claim it was originally made in cobalt as well, but since it has been reissued in cobalt, that color is not as safe for the purist to buy.

Water or lemonade sets, decanter units, tumble ups, and steins with small counterparts are featured in this section. Punch sets are beverage holders as well and are treated with equal respect for they are in high demand.

Punch sets consist of a main bowl and either four or six cups. Only two patterns have been reissued, one of which is Thumbelina or, as it is more commonly called, Flattened Diamond. The other set, called Buzz Star or Whirligig, was an United States Glass Company pattern #15101. Whirligig was a product of a mould-grabbing boo-boo. The original punch bowl mould measures 4¼″ tall and 4⅝″ wide. The new bowl is a jelly compote with a tall stem which results in the measurement being 5⅞″ tall. So far it has been reproduced in crystal and cobalt and with carnival treatment.

The lemonade sets and decanter sets have a main item and either four or six cups or tumblers. At times there is a tray which finishes off the set in style.

Tumble ups are nearly always European and consist of a main bottle and a tumbler which fits over the bottle's neck or, more rarely, down inside the main unit. If a collector is lucky, he or she may find a matching underplate or be treated to a handle, placed for convenience, on the side of the tumbler. Tumble ups are commonly known as night sets.

A rare ruby with enamel glass tea set is shown on the cover of this book and in this section. A second miniature glass tea set, which is European, is presented for the first time. There is also an unusual beaded-glass tea pot, sugar, creamer, spooner with cups and saucers to complete the table setting for the little hostess. The spooner has beaded spoons which add interest to this rare and unusual tea set presentation.

Lemonade or water sets range in price from $100 to $800. Tumble ups may be found for as little as $125 or for as much as $800, depending on the type of glass and its decoration. Stein sets which are not very common may be found for as little as $40 or for as much as $600, depending on the rarity of the item. For instance, the Wabash Grape stein set seems to have been exported from Columbus, Ohio, with very few sets remaining in America. Although one lucky collector recently purchased a complete set for $135, most advanced collectors would pay several hundred dollars for the thrill of adding a complete set to their collections. Punch sets range in price from $75 to $1200, with the medium blue transparent glass Nursery Rhyme set capturing the highest dollar. Decanter sets, except for Mirror, were produced mostly in Europe. They have wonderful treatments of enamel and gold, with delightful sizes and shapes luring collectors to pay high prices for these prizes. There is a wide range of prices in this category from $125 to around $1,000. Glass tea sets are showing themselves at the present time with limited exposure because they are immediately snapped up by eager collectors. Three different sets are featured in this publication.

The guide prices in this section of the text are for complete pieces or units. A price range has been given to accommodate regional differences. Most sets have been priced by the color and piece, as well as by the unit.

Measurements will vary because glassmaking is not exact.

Measurements for the beverage sets were taken as follows:

pitcher—base to pouring spout height

tumbler—base to rim height

tray—diameter

tumble up tumbler—base to rim height

tea pot—base to finial height

cup—base to rim height

creamer—base to pouring spout height

sugar—base to finial height

punch bowl—base to rim height

punch cup—base to rim height

decanter jug—base to rim height

*Reproductions will be explained in the text.

———————

†indicates a particular item has been shown in color and black and white.

*indicates an item has been reproduced.

DECANTER SETS

Figure D-1 ROPE of SAPPHIRE: The special color touch on this Sandwich decanter adds interest to this miniature decanter set.

decanter, 5″ $350-$400.

goblet, 2″ $40-$50.

set for four, $475-$600.

Collection: Lechler

Figure D-2 FRENCH TRAVEL: A special addition to this two-decanter set is a tray and biscuit jar. The design is a fruit and vine motif. This is a rare set for any collection and may be found in its original box.

large decanter, 5½″

small decanter, 3½″

biscuit jar, 3″

goblet, 2″

tray, 5⅝″ across and ¾″ deep

collected as a set, $475-$600.

Collection: Lechler

Figure D-3 TINY TOT KEG: This toy keg set from Czechoslovakia would be a rare addition for any collection. It is marked "Tiny Tot Keg" and has its original stopper and wee faucet. The set is enameled with flowers and is held in its own brass-like holder. This set should be collected as a unit and is priced as such.

keg, 4½″ tall, 3″ long

cup, 1″ tall and 1″ across rim

complete set for four, $325-$450.

Collection: Feltner

Figure D-4 GOLD AND CLEAR: This set came in its own little traveling case with a spot for the decanter and goblets.

decanter, 4½″

goblets, 1⅞″

set for four, $325-$425.

Collection: Lechler

Figure D-5 ENAMELED WITH DOTTED FLOWERS: This glass is so thin it is difficult to carry the set on the original tray without having the goblets tip over.

decanter, 5⅛″

tumblers 1⅛″

tray, 5½″

set for four, $275-$375.

Collection: Lechler

Figure D-6 ENAMELED FLOWERS: This whisk-shaped decanter has six matching goblets. The set is more than likely European because of its small size, and it may have had a tray at one time.

decanter, 4¾″

goblet, 1¾″

set for six, $450-$600.

Collection: Lechler

Figure D-7 THREADED: The threaded stylish circles covering the cruet decanter and small tumblers create an exciting find for miniature collectors. The set has been seen in crystal and cranberry.

decanter, 4½″ ht. $200-$300.

decanter, color $250-$350.

tumbler, 1¾″ $25-$35.

tumbler, color $35-$45.

crystal set for four, $375-$500.

cranberry set for four, $425-$600.

Collection: Mangee

Figure D-8 ENAMELED LEAF AND VINE: This set which is complete with tray and good gold trim has a white enameled motif of leaves and vines.

decanter, 5⅞″ complete $375-$400.

goblet, 2⅞″ $35-$50.

tray, 6⅞″ $100-$125.

set, $500-$800.

Collection: Mangee

Figure D-9 MIRROR AND FAN: The catalogue proof for this American toy decanter set was shown in the 1910 Butler Brothers fall distribution ad display. This "Crystal Gem" was advertised as good crystal with embossed panel designs. One box, with one set in it, cost eighteen cents. A gold-decorated boxed set sold for thirty-five cents in 1914.

decanter, 8¾″ $50-$75.

tumbler, 1⅞″ $8-$10.

set/correct stopper, $150-$175.

Collection: Lechler

Figure D-10 CONTEMPORARY FROSTED: This delicately blown set probably does not have much age, but it is certainly meant for the little hostess.

decanter, $35-$45.

goblet, $12-$15.

set, $75-$135.

Collection: Johnston

Figure D-11 SANDWICH (type): Sandwich or French, the desire to collect this small, choice set is the same. A quilted stopper completes the effect of elegance.

decanter, 4⅞″ $300-$325.

tumbler, 1⅜″ $35-$45.

set for four, $450-$550.

Collection: Lechler

Figure D-12 JOHANNESBURG FROSTED: This tiny decanter set with its matching tray is frosted from base to stopper tip. "Johannesburg" is written in red, with gold circles finishing the flourish.

decanter, $50-$75.

goblet, $25-$30.

tray, $40-$75.

set complete for four, $150-$325.

Collection: Lechler

Figure D-13 SILVER OVER-LAY: This highly decorated decanter set rests well on its irregularly shaped tray. Its busy design consists of silver over clear glass with gold trim. The decanter seems never to have had a stopper.

decanter, 3½″ $75-$100.

cup, 1⅝″ $18-$20.

tray, 5¼″ $35-$75.

set complete for four, $175-$325.

Collection: Feltner

Figure D-14 CLEAR SWIRL: This is a clear swirl, cruet-type decanter and six tumblers.

decanter, $25-$30.

tumbler, $10-$12.

set, $75-$125.

Collection: Mangee

Figure D-15 ENAMELED DOT AND FLOWER: This European (type) decanter set has accents of colorful enamel. (All European Decanter sets should be bought as sets in order to match the unit correctly.)

decanter, 4½″

goblet, 1⅞″

set, $450-$600.

Collection: Landskov

Bohemian miniature decanter set, Figure D-17.

87

Figure D-16 DIMPLED: This rare toy decanter set is thin and delicate. The decanter is dimpled-in-the-mould and carries small enameled flowers. There is a matching tray to this set. This decanter set should be bought as a unit for exact matching purposes.

decanter, just under 4"

footed tumbler, 1¾"

tray, 5"

set, $475-$600.

Collection: Lechler

Figure D-17 BOHEMIAN: This set has a vine and grape motif and is shown in the black and white section of this book. The ornate, original stopper tops off the decanter to perfection. This type of set should be bought in completion because it is difficult to match.

decanter, 6⅜"

stopper alone, 2⅜"

goblet, 3"

tray, 6¼"

set for four, $450-$650.

Figure D-18 ETCHED: The etched decanter set has two different-sized goblets accompanying the fine-lined decanter. The bottle has a mushroom finial. Fine continuous vines and leaves sport a berry motif.

decanter, 5⅜"

small goblet, 2⅓"

larger goblet, 2⅝"

set for six, $450-$650.

photograph by David Grim

Collection: Rosenberger

Etched decanter set, Figure D-18.

Figure D-19 WHEAT SHEAF: This wine set is a Cambridge Glass Company product. There may be two different sizes in this decanter.

decanter, 5¼" $60-$75.

tumbler, 1¾" $12-$18.

set for six, $150-$225.

Collection: Lechler

Lemonade or Water Sets

Nursery Rhyme
L-13

Optic
L-14

Petite
Hobnail
L-17

Pattee
Cross
L-16

Banded
Portland
L-19

Plain
Stiegel (type)
L-22

Petite
Square
L-18

LEMONADE OR WATER SETS

†indicates a particular item has been shown in color and black and white.

*indicates an item has been reproduced.

Figure L-0 CAMBRIDGE NO. 1: toy water set: five pieces, water pitcher and four tumblers; clear; cobalt tumblers have been found; common in clear; not reproduced; for a picture of this set, see the table set section under Cambridge Glass Company contributions.

pitcher, 3⅛″ $25-$35.

tumbler, clear, 1⅞″ $5-$8.

tumbler, cobalt, $12-$25.

clear water set, $50-$75.

Figure L-1 COBALT WITH THISLES: probably European; five to seven piece water set; known in cobalt with white enamel; rare; not reproduced.

pitcher, 4¾″ $125-$150.

tumbler, 1¼″ $30-$35.

set, $275-$325.

Collection: Lechler

Figure L-2† ENAMELED RUFFLED: five to seven piece water set, found at times with a tray; the tray was not shown in the original ad; green or crystal with hand-painted flowers or strawberries; rare in any color or with any design; tumblers are very rare; not reproduced.

water pitcher, 6″ $150-$175.

tumbler, 2¼″ $40-$45.

tray, $65-$75.

set without tray, $375-$450.

Collection: Lechler

Enameled Ruffled lemonade set, Figure L-2.

91

Figures L-3†, TANKARD STYLE: five to seven pieces; clear with enameled flowers or fruit; rare in completion; not reproduced.

tankard pitcher, 5¼″ $135-$160.

tumbler, 2¼″ $40-$45.

set, $375-$450.

Collection: Lechler
    Largent, lily tumblers

L-3   L-3   L-2

Figure L-4† EUROPEAN ENAMELED: slim tankard pitcher with four or six tumblers; clear with heavy enameling; very rare; not reproduced.

pitcher, 3¾″ $150-$200.

tumbler, 1¾″ $40-$60.

set, $450-$600.

Collection: Lechler

L-4

Figure L-5 EUROPEAN ENAMEL: eight piece beverage set; clear with enameled flowers and dots; rare; not reproduced. (See color, page 1).

pitcher, 3″ $200-$300.

tumbler, 1½″ $50-$65.

tray, $75-$100.

set, $600-$800.

Collection: Lechler

Figure L-6† ENAMELED EMERALD MOSER: European, toy water set for two; emerald with heavy enameled flowers; rare; may have other pieces such as a tumble up, candlestick, pomade jars, bowl and jug; not reproduced.

pitcher, 1¾″ $100-$150.

tumbler, 1½″ $50-$75.

set, $200-$350.

Collection: Lechler

Enameled Emerald Moser, Figure L-6.

Figure L-7† GALLOWAY: five to seven piece water set; clear with or without gold trim, blush with or without gold trim; common in clear or clear with gold, rare in good red blush with gold; not reproduced.

pitcher, clear, 3⅞" $28-$38.

pitcher, blush, $100-$150.

tumbler, clear, 2" $5-$7.

tumbler, blush, $20-$25.

clear set, $65-$125.

blush set, $275-$400.

Collection: Lechler

Figure L-8† HOBBS FRANCES WARE: Hobbs, Brockunier and Co.; five to seven piece water set; crystal with amber, frosted with amber, all blue, all amber, all vaseline, white opalescent, all clear, clear with red, frosted with red; rare in completion, very rare with red treatment; not reproduced.

pitcher, 4¾" $150-$200.

pitcher/red, $350-$400.

tumbler, 2¼" $50-$65.

tumbler/red, $75-$125.

sets without red, $450-$650.

set with red, $800-$1000.

Collection: Lechler
            Largent, vaseline

95

Figure L-9 JACOBEAN DOLL'S boxed water set: with a pitcher and six tumblers; Czechoslovakia; available; not reproduced.

pitcher, 1½″

tumbler, ¾″

boxed set, $145-$175.

Collection: Lechler

DOLL'S HOUSE WATERSET IN JACOBEAN GLASSWARE JUG AND SIX TUMBLERS. Made in Czecho-Slovakia.

Little Jo lemonade set, Figure L-10.

Figure L-10†* LITTLE JO, Arched Panels: Westmoreland; five to seven piece water set; old sets in crystal, amber, light pink, light green, perhaps cobalt although the set has been reproduced in cobalt; common in clear, rare in old colors; reproduced.

pitcher, clear, 3¾" $40-$60.

pitcher, old color, $125-$150.

tumbler, clear, 2" $7-$8.

tumbler, old color, $35-$40.

clear set, $80-$125.

old color set, $375-$400.

Collections: Walters, green; Lechler, others.

Figure L-11† MARY GREGORY: five to seven pieces; amber; blue with white figures; very rare; not reproduced.

pitcher, 4½" $300-$350.

tumbler, 2½" $50-$75.

set, $600-$1000.

Collection: Lechler

Figure L-12 MICHIGAN, Loop and Pillar, #15077: United States Glass Company; five to seven piece water set; clear, clear with gold; common; not reproduced.

pitcher, 4" $30-$40.

tumbler, 2⅛" $7-$8.

set, $75-$125.

Mary Gregory lemonade set, Figure L-11.

Michigan lemonade set, Figure L-12.

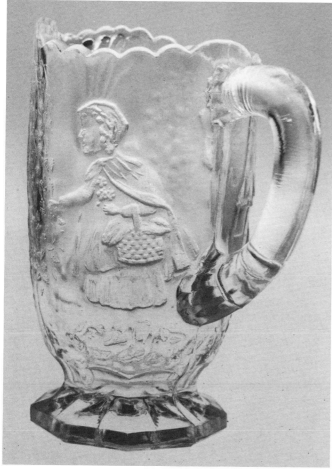

Nursery Rhyme lemonade set, Figure L-13.

Figure L-13† NURSERY RHYME: United States Glass Company; five to seven piece water set as well as a table set, punch set and berry set; clear; water set is available but still desirable; not reproduced.

pitcher, 4¼" $125-$175.

tumbler, 2" $25-$28.

set, $225-$375.

Collection: Lechler

Figure L-14 OPTIC #15091: United States Glass Company; clear; not often seen in completion; not reproduced.

pitcher, 4" $50-$85.

tumbler, 2" $10-$12.

set, $125-$150.

Collection: Lechler

Figure L-15† OVAL STAR Crystal No. 300: Indiana Glass Co.; five to seven piece water set, tray four piece table set, five to seven piece berry set, five to seven piece punch set; clear water set with or without gold; available; not reproduced.

pitcher, 4¼" $85-$100.

tumbler, 2⅜" $12-$15.

tray, 7¼" $100-$125.

set without tray, $150-$200.

set with tray, $200-$300.

Collection: Lechler

Optic #15091 lemonade, Figure L-14.

65¢   **Post paid**

Imitation Cut Glass Water Set

These pieces look exactly like mother's and it will make you feel happy to have them, in your little buffet, ready to serve your guests. Consists of **four** 2-inch high cut glass design glass tumblers, 7½-inch glass tray with beautiful cut glass style design and a 4⅝-inch heavy glass pitcher. **49D1904**
Postpaid **65c**

Oval Star lemonade set, Figure L-15.

100

Figure L-16 PATTEE CROSS: United States Glass Company; five to seven piece water set, five to seven piece berry set, possibly punch set; clear with or without gold; available; not reproduced.

pitcher, 4½″ $75-$100.

tumbler, 1¾″ $15-$18.

set, $175-$225.

Collection: Lechler

Figure L-17 PETITE HOBNAIL: five to seven piece water set, tumble up using a tumbler from this set, tray; amber, blue, clear; very rare; not reproduced.

pitcher, clear, 4¾″ $150-$175.

pitcher, color, $200-$300.

tumbler, 2³/₁₃″ $30-$35.

tray, 6½″ x 7¾″ $200-$225.

clear set with tray, $550-$650.

color set with tray, $650-$900.

Collection: Lechler

Figure L-18 PETITE SQUARE: five to seven piece water set; clear; supposed to use the same tumblers as Petite Hobnail; no catalogue proof that this is a toy set; not reproduced.

pitcher, 3¼″ $75-$100.

tumbler, 2³⁄₁₆″ $30-$35.

set, $175-$225.

Collection: Mangee, pitcher

Figure L-19 PORTLAND BANDED: five to seven piece water set; clear with or without gold; available; not reproduced.

pitcher, 3½″ $30-$60.

tumbler, 2¼″ $10-$12.

set, $75-$125.

Collection: Feltner

**L-19
Portland
Banded**

Figure L-20 PORTLAND: five to seven piece water set; clear with or without gold; available; not reproduced.

pitcher, 4″ $25-$40.

tumbler, 2⅛″ $7-$8.

set, $70-$100.

Collection: Lechler

Figure L-21 REX, Fancy Cut: Co-operative Flint Glass Company; five to seven piece water set; four piece table set; five to seven piece punch set; clear; avaiable; not reproduced.

pitcher, 3½″ $75-$125.

tumbler, 1½″ $15-$22.

set, $175-$200.

Collection: Lechler

L-20
Portland

L-21
Rex

Figure L-22 STIEGEL (type): five to seven piece doll's house water set; available; not reproduced.

pitcher, 3″ $25-$40.

tumbler, 1¼″ $10-$12.

set, $75-$90.

Collection: Lechler

Figure L-23 COLONIAL FLUTE: Lancaster Glass Company; five to seven piece water set, five to seven piece berry set; five to seven piece punch set; common; not reproduced. (not pictured)

pitcher, 3¼″ $25-$35.

tumbler, 2″ $5-$8.

set, $50-$75.

L-22
Stiegel

PUNCH SETS

Figure P-1† CAMBRIDGE INVERTED STRAWBERRY: *five to seven piece punch set, five to seven piece berry set; clear only, in the old items; punch set reproduced by Mosser of Cambridge, Ohio, in many colors; old clear punch set is available; berry set is difficult to complete and has not been reproduced to date.

old punch bowl, 3⅜″ $50-$125.

old punch cup, 1⅛″ $20-$22.

old punch set, $150-$225.

new punch set, $20-$40.

Collection: Lechler

P-1
Cambridge
Inverted
Strawberry

Figure P-2 BUZZ STAR #15101, Whirligig: United States Glass Company; four piece table set, *five to seven piece punch set; clear; green and clambroth spooners have been recorded; common in clear; reproduced punch set using incorrect punch bowl mould.

old punch bowl, 4¼″ $40-$50.

new punch bowl, 5⅞″ $10-$16.

punch cup, 1¼″ $6-$8.

old punch set, $75-$100.

new punch set, $16-$25.

15101 Toy Punch Set, 7 Pieces
$3.00 per doz.
Packed one set in pasteboard box
Gold Decorated, $6.60 per doz.

Buzz
Star
#15101

Figure P-3 CAMBRIDGE WHEAT SHEAF No. 2660: five to seven piece punch set, five to seven piece berry set, five to seven piece decanter set; clear; all available, but the decanter set is more difficult to locate; not reproduced.

Figure P-3 punch bowl, 3½″ $30-$40.

Figure P-3 punch cup, 1¼″ $7-$8.50.

Figure P-3 punch set, $75-$100.

Figure D-19 wine jug, 5¼″ $60-$75.

Figure D-19 tumbler, 1¾″ $12-$18.

Figure D-19 wine set, $150-$225.

Collection: Johnston, punch set; Lechler, wine set.

Figure D-19
Cambridge
Wheat Sheaf

Figure P-3
Cambridge
Wheat Sheaf No. 2660

Figure P-4 CHATEAU No. 714: New Martinsville; five to seven piece punch set; table set; punch set is very rare; not reproduced.

punch bowl, 3⅜″ $350-$400.

punch cup, 1¼″ $30-$40.

punch set, $400-$600.

Collection: Johnston

Figure P-5 COLONIAL: Lancaster Glass Company; five to seven piece punch set; five to seven piece water set; five to seven piece berry set; clear; common; not reproduced.

punch bowl, 3³/₁₆″ $40-$60.

punch cup, 1⅞″ $13-$15.

punch set, $125-$150.

Collection: Lechler

No. 714 Toy Punch Set
Chateau

P-4 Chateau No. 714

P-5
Colonial

107

Figure P-6† NURSERY RHYME: four piece table set, five to seven piece water set, five to seven piece punch set, five to seven piece berry set; all clear except for the punch set which comes in white or blue milkglass and crystal or medium blue transparent glass; both blue punch sets are rare, with the medium blue transparent being the rarest punch set in toy glass collections; not reproduced.

punch bowl, clear, 3⅜″ $150-$200.

punch bowl, blue milkglass, $300-$400.

punch bowl, blue transparent, $400-$500.

punch cup, clear, 1⅜″, $20-$25.

punch cup, blue milkglass, $35-$45.

punch cup, blue transparent, $50-$75.

clear or white milkglass set, $250-$400.
blue milkglass set, $600-$700.
medium blue transparent set, $800-$1500.
Collections: Johnston, blue transparent; Lechler, others.

Figure P-7 OVAL STAR No. 3001: Indiana Glass Company; four piece table set, five to seven piece punch set, five to seven piece berry set, five to seven piece water set with two different sizes of pitchers; water set sometimes sold with a tray; clear with or without gold; available; not reproduced.

punch bowl, 4⅜″ tall, 4½″ dia. $50-$60.

punch cup, 1⅛″ $10-$12.

punch set, $100-$125.

Collection: Ad

P-7
Oval
Star

P-6
Nursery
Rhyme

Figure P-8 PATTEE CROSS: United States Glass Company; five to seven piece water set; five to seven piece berry set, five to seven piece punch set; crystal with or without gold; punch set is difficult to assemble; not reproduced.

punch bowl, 2⅝″ $125-$150.

punch cup, 1¼″ $30-$40.

punch set, $300-$375.

Collection: Feltner, bowl
Lechler, cup

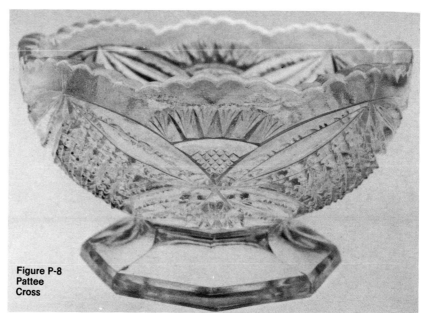

Figure P-8
Pattee
Cross

Figure P-9 REX, Fancy Cut: Co-operative Flint Glass Company; four piece table set, five to seven piece punch set, five to seven piece water set; punch set is difficult to complete, other sets are available; clear with or without gold; not reproduced.

punch bowl, 4⅜″ $150-$200.

punch cup, 1¼″ $30-$35.

punch set, $375-$425.

Collection: Lechler

Figure P-10†* THUMBELINA, Flattened Diamond; *four piece table set, *five to seven piece punch set; old table sets in clear and some color, old punch sets in clear; heavily reproduced in color.

punch bowl, 4¼″ $30-$40.

punch cup, 1⅜″ $5-$8.

punch set, old clear $60-$100.

punch set, old color $150-$225.

Collection: Lechler

P-9
Rex

Figure P-10   Thumbelina, Flattened Diamond

Figure P-11 TULIP AND HONEYCOMB: Wabash Series; Federal Glass Company, Columbus, Ohio; four piece table set plus an extra butter, five to seven piece punch set, four piece vegetable set; clear punch set is common; not reproduced.

punch bowl, 4¼″ $30-$40.

punch cup, 1¼″ $8-$10.

punch set, $80-$100.

Collection: Ad

Figure P-12† WILD ROSE: four piece table set, five to seven piece punch set, candlestick; punch set in white milkglass with or without paint, crystal; punch set is very rare in clear, available in milkglass; not reproduced.

punch bowl, clear, 4¼″ $150-$250.

punch bowl, milkglass, $50-$60.

punch cup, clear, 1¼″, $20-$30.

punch cup, milkglass, $10-$18.

clear punch set, $300-$450.

milkglass punch set, $100-$175.

Collection: Haskell, clear bowl; Mangee, milkglass punch set.

Tulip and
Honeycomb

Punch Bowl

Figure P-11

Punch Cup
—55—

Figure P-11

P-12
Wild Rose

STEIN SETS

Figure S-1 GRAPE STEIN SET: Wabash series; Federal Glass Company, Columbus, Ohio; main stein and four or six small steins; clear or clear with paint; very rare; not reproduced.

main stein, $200-$275.

small stein, 1½" $50-$75.

set, $400-$600.

Collection: Haskell, main stein; Lechler, small stein.

Figure S-2 MICHIGAN STEIN SET: pattern also known in table and water sets, nappy; stein set has main stein and four or six small candy-dip-style counterparts; clear or clear with gold; available; not reproduced, (See miscellaneous color, Page 14.)

main stein, 2⅞" $30-$40.

small stein, 2" $10-$12.

set, $60-$125.

Collection: Mangee

Figure S-1 Grape Stein Set

Stein Set

Figure S-2 Michigan Stein Set

Figure S-3 MONK STEIN SET: clear or milkglass with or without color; available in milkglass, a little more scarce in clear glass; not reproduced.

main stein, clear, 2⅞″ $60-$75.

main stein, milkglass, $45-$65.

small stein, clear, 2⅛″ $30-$35.

small stein, milkglass $20-$25.

clear set, $200-$350.

milkglass set, $160-$275.

Collection: Largent

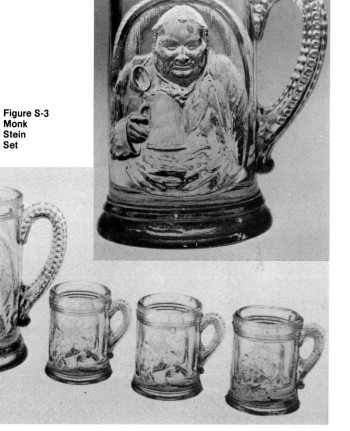

Figure S-3
Monk
Stein
Set

GLASS TEA SETS

Figure TEA-1† RUBY WITH ENAMEL: possibly European; should be collected as nearly complete as possible because of matching; rare; not reproduced; see cover and color plate.

tea pot, 5"

creamer, 3"

cup, 2"

Figure TEA-1

saucer, 3½"

setting for two, $350-$500.

Collection: Lechler

Figure TEA-2 BEADED GLASS: tea set for two; unusual with white and blue glass beads forming the pieces; this unit should be collected as a set because it would be impossible to match; not reproduced. (See color, Page 15.)

tea pot, 3¼"

sugar, 2¾"

creamer 2¼"

spooner, 2"

cup, 1½"

saucer, 2¼"

set, $150-$250.

Collection: Lechler

Figure TEA-3 CLEAR WITH ENAMEL AND GOLD: tea set; European; should be collected as a set; rare; not reproduced. (See color, Page 14.)

tea pot, 3½"

creamer, 1¼"

covered sugar, 2"

cup, 1⅛"

saucer, 2"

set for two, $400-$500.

Collection: Lechler

TUMBLE UPS

Figure TU-1 blue transparent glass with enameled flowers and trim; 4¼" complete; Mangee collection: $275-$325.

Figure TU-2 ornate cranberry with lavish enamel design; 4¼"; Lechler collection: $625-$675.

Figure TU-3 pink cased with ruffled lip on jug, enameled design in relief; 3½"; Lechler collection; $325-$400.

Figure TU-4 art glass cobalt three piece night set with heavy gold and colorful flowers in blue, rose, yellow, orange and green; jug unit, 4½", plate 5½"; Lechler collection; $650-$700.

Figure TU-5 Clambroth, gold-ringed trim, flora design in gold on tumbler base; 3"; Lechler collection; $160-$175.

Figure TU-6 tiny art glass tumble up in cobalt with runs of heavy gold and accents of enamel; jug unit, 3½", under plate, 3"; Lechler collection; $500-$600.

Figure TU-7 sapphire with handle; enamel accents; 4"; Lechler collection; $275-$375.

Figure TU-8 Bohemian glass with a modified stem, etched all over with wooded scenes and deer; mushroom-shaped stopper; 5"; Lechler collection; $350-$375.

Figure TU-9 ruby glass with a wooded scene with dogs and birds etched on the glass; the flat-topped stopper is ruby; 4¼"; Lechler collection; $350-$375.

Figure TU-10 hour-glass-shaped miniature tumble up; clear glass with ruby stain; etched designs and birds; 2½"; Lechler collection; $275-$325.

Figure TU-11 cranberry glass with heavy enameled flowers and butterflies, large amounts of gold; 3¾"; Lechler collection; $400-$500.

Figure TU-12 Bohemian glass with pictures and writing; stopper; 3⅜"; Lechler collection; $225-$250.

Figure TU-13 cut honeycomb design on clear body with ruby stain; grape, flower and leaf design; stopper; 4¼"; Lechler collection; $300-$375.

Figure TU-14 clear glass with ruby decorative flashing; 4⅞"; Freshour collection; $200-$300.

Figure TU-15 crystal glass with a chain of enameled circles and dots; 4⅜"; Lechler collection; $250-$350.

Figure TU-16 tiny clear glass tumble up and under plate with heavy enameled flowers and leaves; jug unit 2⅝", under plate 2½"; Lechler collection; $350-$450.

Figure TU-17 five piece art glass dresser set including: tumble up, candlestick, jug and bowl, and puff jar; green glass with heavy enameled miniature flowers; jug, 3", bowl, 1½" tall, 2" across, tumble up 2½", puff jar, 1½" tall; Lechler collection; candlestick, Largent collection; jug and bowl, $100-$150; tumble up, $300-$400; candlestick, $75-$100; puff jar, $75-$125.

Figure TU-18 over-shot glass with stippled, frosted style; clover leaf design with gold accents; 2¼"; Lechler collection; $100-$150.

Figure TU-19 over-shot glass with stippled, frosted style, all over blue dots; 2¼"; Lechler collection; $100-$150.

Figure TU-20 rippled-shape in clear glass with gold trim and enameled accents in red, green and white; 3½"; Lechler collection; $125-$160.

Figure TU-21 Mary Gregory light blue tumble up, 1½"; Lechler collection; $350-$400.

Figure TU-22 cobalt with enameled flowers; 3"; Maag collection; $450-$500.

Figure TU-23 clear paneled tumble up with red, orange and yellow enameled flowers; 3"; Lechler collection; $325-$375.

Figure TU-24 blue swirl, no decorations; 3⅛"; Lechler collection; $125-$150.

Figure TU-25 art deco style, paneled tumble up with red, blue and gold designs on a clear body; just under 5"; Lechler collection; $400-$450.

Figure TU-26 cranberry with heavy white enamel enhanced with gold accents; 4"; Lechler collection; $375-$400.

Figure TU-27 amethyst without decoration; 5⅜"; Lechler collection; $200-$275.

Figure TU-28 canary without decoration; 5⅜"; Lechler collection; $200-$275.

Figure TU-29 green opaline without decoration; 5"; Lechler collection; $325-$350.

Figure TU-30 pink tumble up with black handle; tumbler fitting inside the neck of the pitcher; 5"; $350-$400.

Figure TU-31 blue pitcher with etched flowers, yellow handle; tumbler fitting inside the neck of the pitcher; 5"; Lechler collection; $350-$400.

Figure TU-32 citrus green pitcher with a black handled tumbler fitting inside the neck of the pitcher; 5"; Lechler collection; $350-$400.

Figure TU-33 flare-bottomed cobalt with white enamel; 4½"; Lechler collection; $375-$400.

Figure TU-34 white coin-spot; 3¼"; Lechler collection; $325-$400.

Figure TU-35 French blue clambroth with underplate and delicate gold accents; deep underplate; jug unit 4", plate, 4½" diameter, 1" height; Lechler collection; $600-$650.

Figure TU-36 clear paneled with gold trim and green leaves with white flowers; 4⅞"; Lechler collection; $150-$200.

Figure TU-37 blue hobnail using the same tumbler as those found in the Petite Hobnail water set; jug 3¾" tall, tumbler, 2³⁄₁₆"; Lechler collection; $350-$425.

Figure TU-38 cobalt swirl, rough pontil on both pieces; 5"; Lechler collection; $125-$175.

Figure TU-39 canary Mary Gregory; 4¾"; Lechler collection; $450-$525.

Figure TU-40 cranberry Mary Gregory; also known in apple green; 3⅛"; Lechler collection; $450-$525.

Figure TU-41 cobalt Mary Gregory pitcher matching the 1½" cobalt tumble up; both are also known in light blue; tumble up; Lechler collection; $350-$525.

Figure TU-41A pitcher, Mrs. Lyle Welker collection; $100-$150.

Figure TU-42 white twist art glass tumble up with under plate; 3″ jug unit, 3″ plate; Lechler collection; $450-$525.

Figure TU-43 two-toned blue twist tumble up with under plate; 3⅛″ jug unit, 3⅛″ graduated depth under plate; Lechler collection; $450-$525.

Figure TU-44 lutz-style blue and white twist tumble up; 3⅞″; Lechler collection; $450-$525.

Figure TU-45 rich yellow cased glass tumble up with peach enamel; 4″; Lechler collection; $275-$375.

MINIATURE CANDLESTICKS

Many of the glasshouses of the past produced miniature candlesticks. Heisey did a particularly good job of it. A few of their finest have been reproduced, but there are still some grand ones to collect if you are looking for old chambersticks or candlesticks.

The Heisey factory made four single-socket toy candlesticks. Their #31 is a toy chamberstick which has a handle that does not touch the candle cup. (The chambersticks having handles touching the socket are considered to belong to Duncan and Miller.) The #31 Heisey stick is the only style to receive the special color treatments of moonbeam, flamingo, and sahara. This style was reissued by Westmoreland without a Heisey mark in clear glass. Heisey's #31 is listed in this publication as C-25.

Heisey's #33, C-21, was made in standard sizes as well. They come in 5″, 7″ and 9″ offerings. The Heisey mark is found on one of the side panels below the neck. It was originally made in clear glass. This candlestick was reissued by Imperial in crystal and green.

Heisey's #30, C-20, was made only in crystal and marked on the underside of the base.

The five-inch Heisey #5 candlestick is marked on the underside of its hollow base. Both the top and base have six sides. Heisey's #5 is C-17 in this publication.

Sandwich candlesticks date from 1850-1870 in the toy line. Sandwich produced a special little candlestick with a candle cup which would hold the tip of a small finger. McKee and Brothers also fashioned the same six-paneled design with an identical hexagonal base, finishing it off with six flutes on its round rim. The Sandwich or McKee candlestick is 1⅝″ tall. There is a New England Glass Company candlestick which is 2″ tall and has a socket that could carry a candle smaller than today's birthday candles.

Companies often bought moulds from commercial mould makers and filled the moulds with their own glass. Even with catalogue proof, it is not safe to state that only one company produced a particular product. The commercial mould makers sold many moulds of the same, or nearly the same, design to many different factories. As long as they sold, the mould companies did not really care who filled them with glass. This makes definite attribution to any one company very difficult. It is best to simply enjoy this collection while you are digging for clues.

When the book CHILDREN'S GLASS DISHES was published by Thomas Nelson, I thought that giving numbers to candlesticks would help collectors and dealers catalogue and sell their ware more easily. I have carried these numbers to this, the fourth book, and it has not been easy. One may easily recognize a candlestick while holding it, but after some printers finish with the original pictures, it is very difficult to identify the small ware. Nevertheless, the tradition is continued here with a few adjustments and some new "C" numbers added.

CANDLESTICKS

The candlesticks are described starting with each top row and moving from left to right. The "C" numbers are carried from my previous books: CHILDREN'S GLASS DISHES; CHILDREN'S GLASS DISHES, CHINA AND FURNITURE, Vol. I; CHILDREN'S GLASS DISHES, CHINA, AND FURNITURE, Vol. II. Any new candlesticks added to this publication will receive new "C" numbers. All candlesticks are known only in clear unless noted. The price range is given for individual pieces. The candlesticks in this section are from the Lechler collection unless noted. An * will indicate an item has been reproduced.

Top Row:
Figure C-15 4″; $60-$75.
Figure C-8 4″; etched flowers; $50-$75.

Figure C-16* 4⅝″; Heisey's #5; $75-$85.
Figure C-17 4⅜″; Heisey's #5; $75-$85.
Figure C-18 4¼″; $60-$75.
Figure C-14 4¼″; $75-$80.
Figure C-10 3½″; $75-$100.

Middle Row:
Figure C-15 4″; $50-$75.
Figure C-20 3⅝″; Heisey's #30; $50-$75.
Figure C-0 2½″ $50-$70.
Figure C-34 1⅝″ Sandwich; also shown in McKEE VICTORIAN GLASS catalogue reprints from 1859/60 to 1871; $100-$125 in clear; $200-$300 color
Figure C-55 ¾″; Feltner collection; $50-$75.
Figure C-41 1¾″, King Co. #143; Feltner collection; $50-$70.
Figure C-50 2¾″, Sandwich attribution; Largent collection; $175-$200.
Figure C-21* 3″; Heisey's #33; $40-$60.
Figure C-23 3″; Indiana Glass Co.; $30-$40.
Figure C-11 3⅝″; $75-$100.

Bottom Row:
Figure C-52 1½″; dark amethyst lacy; Feltner collection; $60-$80.
Figure C-43 2″; sapphire lacy; $60-$80.
Figure C-24 2″; four candlesticks shown from New England Glass Co.; clear, $60-$75; color $75-$125.
Figure C-32 1″; three chambersticks shown from the New England Glass Co.; yellow, orange, blue bases, also known in rose; $50-$75.

CANDLESTICKS

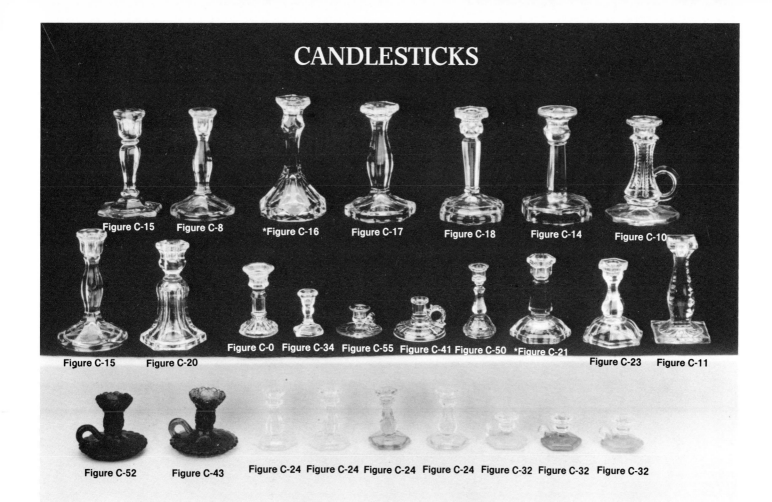

Figure C-15 Figure C-8 *Figure C-16 Figure C-17 Figure C-18 Figure C-14 Figure C-10

Figure C-0 Figure C-34 Figure C-55 Figure C-41 Figure C-50 *Figure C-21

Figure C-15 Figure C-20 Figure C-23 Figure C-11

Figure C-52 Figure C-43 Figure C-24 Figure C-24 Figure C-24 Figure C-24 Figure C-32 Figure C-32 Figure C-32

119

CANDLESTICKS

Top Row:

Figure C-53 4″; $50-$75.

Figure C-36 3⅝″; $40-$60.

Figure C-54* 3″; blue or white milkglass green or crystal; those with "M" have been reproduced; old $150-$200. (3) samples are shown.

Figure C-37 3⅝″; $30-$40.

Figure C-35 4¼″; Wild Rose; $125-$175.

Middle Row:

Figure C-26* 1⅞″; clear and color; $40-$60.

Figure C-25* 2″; Heisey's #31; clear and color; $60-$150.

Figure C-26* 1⅞″; clear and color; $40-$60.

Figure C-29 2″; lacy white milkglass; $40-$60.

Figure C-26 1⅞″; old color; $100-$150.

Figure C-28 2¼″; KRYS-TOL; $30-$50.

Figure C-42 2¼″; clear or color; $30-$50.

Bottom Row:

Figure C-56 3⅝″; mercury glass; $40-$70.

Figure C-57 4″; clear and color; Feltner collection; $40-$60.

Figure C-58 3½″; French; milkglass colors; different from C-5; $30-$40.

Figure C-34

Figure C-22 2⅞″; C-34 and C-22 are the same candlestick with different treatments; $30-$50.

Figure C-59 3¾″; cobalt with enameled birds; Feltner collection; $50-$60.

Figure C-46 3¾″; candy container and candlestick combination; $40-$60.

Figure C-53   Figure C-36   *Figure C-54   Figure C-54   Figure C-54   Figure C-37   Figure C-35

*Figure C-26   *Figure C-25   *Figure C-26   Figure C-29   Figure C-26   Figure C-28   Figure C-42

Figure C-56   Figure C-57   Figure C-58   Figure C-34   Figure C-22   Figure C-59   Figure C-46

Top Row:

Figure C-1* 4⅜″; clear and color; $40-$75; clear shown with two different base styles.

Middle Row:

Figure C-45 7½″; rare hurricane peg lamps with embossed dots and birds; $600-$800 a pair.

Middle and Bottom Rows:

Figure C-19 4¼″; clear and color; rare in color; Feltner and Largent collections; $75-$125.

Middle Row, Center:

Figure C-60 6½″ tallest point, 5″ at shortest candle point; amber; very rare; probably French; should have prisms hanging from each of the four arms; $300-$400 each.

Bottom Row, Center:

Figure C-2 4¾″ center post, 4″ outer branches; four socket; very rare; $150-$175.

Bottom Row, Last:

Figure C-3 4¼″; Laragent collection; $50-$80.

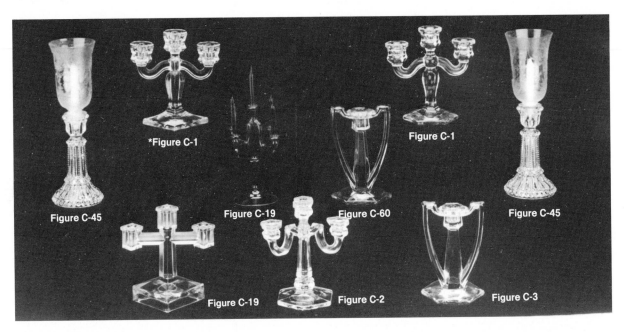

CARNIVAL KITTENS
by Fenton

The Carnival Kitten items are from the Rogers, Walters, Mangee and Largent collections.

Figure CK-1, ruffled dish with four points; 4¼"; marigold, $100-$150; other colors, $300-$400.

Figure CK-2, cup; 2⅛", saucer, 4½"; marigold, $100-$125 per set; clear, $100-$125 per set; other colors, $350-$450 per set.

Figure CK-3, dish; 4¼"; marigold, $150-$175; other colors, $250-$350.

Figure CK-4, ruffled six-point dish; 4¼"; marigold, $150-$175; other colors, $250-$350.

Figure CK-5, vase, 2⅜"; marigold, $200-$250; other colors, $350-$400.

Figure CK-6, cereal bowl; 3½"; marigold, $100-$150; other colors, $250-$375.

Figure CK-7, banana dish, 4⅝"; marigold, $150-$175; other colors, $250-$350.

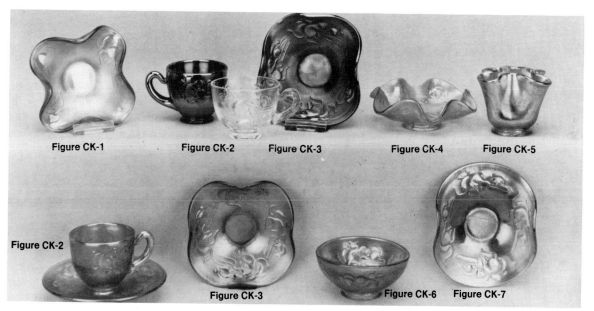

Figure CK-1   Figure CK-2   Figure CK-3   Figure CK-4   Figure CK-5

Figure CK-2   Figure CK-3   Figure CK-6   Figure CK-7

CASTOR SETS

The Victorian toy castor sets are among the earliest units of pleasure offered to today's collector of American miniature glass.

The bottles in the particular holders shown in this publica- tion have been exchanged innumerable times during their marketing history. It is really only safe to speculate that the marked and dated Centennial holder should carry a version of the American Shield bottles and that the Sherwood castor set has at least two differently designed holders. Two different Sherwood boxes have been seen by this author, with only one being shown in this text.

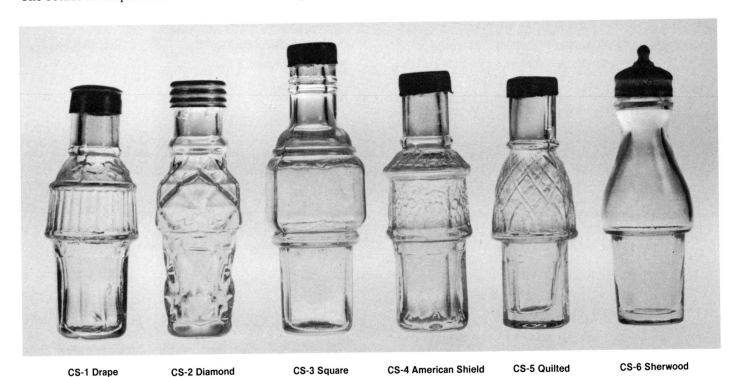

CS-1 Drape   CS-2 Diamond   CS-3 Square   CS-4 American Shield   CS-5 Quilted   CS-6 Sherwood

Three interesting facts about castor sets have been literally unearthed since my last publication. Barlow and Kaiser, well recognized authors in the field of Sandwich glass, stated in their GUIDE TO SANDWICH GLASS *Witch Balls, Containers and Toys,* that they have dug shards of the Ribbon Band castor set, the Sherwood bottles and a blown-moulded-paneled toy castor bottle at the site of the Boston and Sandwich Glass Company. They date these bottles from 1870-1897. After the demise of the Boston and Sandwich Glass Company other companies produced ware on the same site. One must remember, too, that many other glass factories in the East and Midwest produced identical toy castor bottles which copied the standard-size ware used by Mother. The functional use for castor sets was to bring condiments to the table.

There are at least ten different patterns in toy bottles with slight variations in size or mould designs. The metal Victorian holders vary in style much more than the bottles they carry. The holes for the bottles count from two to five. The price range runs from $50 to $200 depending on the condition of the entire unit and whether the bottles have their original stoppers, caps or corks.

CASTOR SETS

The bottle holders will not always carry the same patterned bottles. The stoppers and caps may not be original in all of the pictures. The prices indicate complete sets in the best possible condition.

The castor sets are from the Largent and Lechler collections. The sterling silver holder, see color CS-4, is from the Haskell collection.

Figure CS-1, DRAPE; $125-$150.

Figure CS-2, DIAMOND; $125-$140.

Figure CS-3, SQUARE; $130-$140.

Figure CS-4, AMERICAN SHIELD: clear bottles in dated holder, $150-$200; cobalt bottles in dated holder, $200-$400; clear bottles in sterling silver holder, $125-$175; American Shield's design and size will vary.

Figure CS-5, QUILTED; $75-$125.

Figure CS-6, SANDWICH SHERWOOD; two different holders: two-bottled set in original box, $60-$100; four-bottled set in original box, $150-$175.

Figure CS-7, SANDWICH RIBBON BAND; several sizes, some design variation; $75-$100.

Figure CS-8, FLUTED; may be sandwich; difficult to find; $100-$125.

Figure CS-9, CIRCLE-IN-SQUARE; $100-$160.

Figure CS-10, SANDWICH blown bottles complete with fittings, $150-$225.

Figure CS-11, PLAIN PATTERN BLOWN; double bottles; blown; with proper fittings; $75-$100.

Figure CS-12, PLAIN PATTERN BLOWN in revolving holder; when complete with proper fittings; $125-$150.

Figure CS-1 Drape

Figure CS-2 Diamond

126

Figure CS-3 Square

Figure CS-4 American Shield

127

Figure CS-5 Quilted

Figure CS-6 Sandwich Sherwood

128

Figure CS-7 Ribbon Band

Figure CS-9 Circle-In-Square

129

CS-10 Sandwich Glass castor set

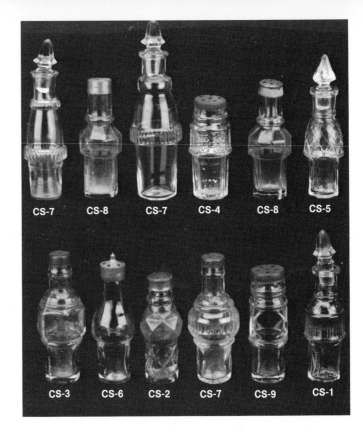

CS-7 CS-8 CS-7 CS-4 CS-8 CS-5

CS-3 CS-6 CS-2 CS-7 CS-9 CS-1

CHAMBER SETS

The Chamber Sets have been shown in color and black and white.

Figure CH-2, EUROPEAN clear glass with blue enamel decorations; rare in glass; small bowl, 1½" tall, 3" dia; large bowl 1¾" tall, 4¼" dia; pitcher, 3½"; holder, 2" long; collection: Lechler; $500-$600.

Figure CH-1, DUTCH BOUDOIR, bowl, 1³/₁₆", *candlestick, 3", chamber pot, 2⅛", pitcher, 2¼", pomade/lid, 1½", slop jar, 2⅛", tray, 3¾" x 6"; very rare in green or clear, also produced in blue or white milkglass; collections: green, Welker; other, Lechler.

green or clear tray, $300-$400.

green or clear candlestick, $200-$250.

green or clear pomade, $275-$350.

green or clear covered potty, pitcher or bowl, $200-$300 each.

complete set in green or clear: $1,500-$2,000.

milkglass tray, $200-$350. (white milkglass tray is difficult to find).

*milkglass candlestick, $150-$175.

milkglass pomade with lid, $150-$175. (white milkglass pomades are difficult to find).

milkglass covered potty, pitcher or bowl, $150-$175 each.

complete blue or white milkglass set, $800-$1,000.

Dutch Boudoir potty, dresser set, and slop jar CH-1

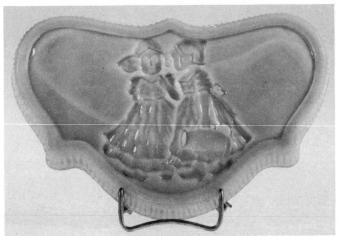

**Dutch Boudoir
dresser tray
CH-1**

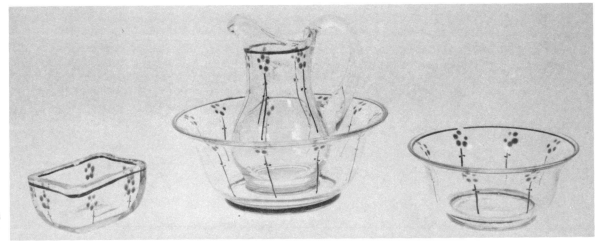

**English glass
chamber set
CH-2**

132

CONDIMENT AND CAKE

Figure COND-1, ENGLISH HOBNAIL condiment set; Westmoreland Specialty Co; 1924; milkglass, clear, green; vinegar cruet, 2⅞″, pepper, 3¼″, salt, ⅞″, tray, 5″; collection: Largent; $40-$50.

Figure COND-2, CROSS HATCHING, condiment set; salt, cruet, shaker; collection: Haskell; $40-$75.

Figure COND-3, PLANET, condiment set; vinegar cruet, 3″, pepper, 3¼″, salt, 1″, tray, 2½″ x 6″; collection: Largent; $90-$125.

Figure COND-4, HICKMAN condiment set; clear, green, rare in blue; vinegar cruet, 3″; pepper 3½″; salt, 1″; tray, 3¼″ x 5″; collection: Largent; clear, $50-$70, green, $70-$100; blue $125-$175.

CUPS AND SAUCERS

Figure CUP-1, blue swirl design with gold-trim footed cup, 1¼″, saucer, 2½″; possibly French; collection: Feltner; $20-$25.

Figure CUP-2, CAT AND DOG, amber, blue or clear cup, 2″, saucer, 3½″; two pictures in a beaded frame of a dog in a garden and a cat; collection: Largent; $85-$95.

Figure CUP-3, blue milkglass DIAMONDS cup, 1⅞″ x 2¾″ and saucer, 3¾″; collection: Lechler; $90-$100.

Figure CUP-4, FACE cup 2½″ x 2½⅝″; amber, blue, clear; collection: Largent; $40-$50.

Figure CUP-5, OPALESCENT LACE, cup and saucer, collection: Largent; $40-$60.

Figure CUP-6, STIPPLED LEAF AND GRAPE, large leaf with grape clusters on each side of cup, 1¾″ tall, the saucer has the leaf and grape appearing four times; collection: Lechler; $25-$30.

Figure CUP-7, FRENCH heavy, thick glass with panels and large oval looped tears; cup, 1⅞″ tall, saucer is 2½″ diameter; collection: Mangee; $30-$40.

Figure CUP-8, DOG MEDALLION cup, 1¾″ tall, saucer 3½″ diameter, dog with long ears; collection: Lechler; $75-$125.

Figure CUP-9, star in a circle with heavy beaded work cup and saucer; clear and possibly color; collection: Largent; $30-$50.

Figure CUP-10, DAISY BAND, cup, 2½″ x 2½″; amber, blue, clear; collection: Largent; $35-$50.

Figure CUP-11, BASKET WEAVE, cup 2½″ x 2⅝″, saucer; amber, blue clear; collection: Largent; $35-$50.

Figure CUP-12, LION; clear, frosted, clear/frosted heads; collection: Lechler; $50-$125.

Figure CUP-13, WEE BRANCHES; collection: Lechler; $50-$75.

EPERGNES

The epergnes are shown in the color plate section. The descriptions read from the top row, left to right.

Figure E-1, rare compote, epergne combination in miniature epergne, 6½"; (2) matching compotes, 2½"; collection: Walters; three-piece set; $275-$400.

Figure E-2, two-piece clear glass item with etching; 6⅞" collection: Mangee; $50-$60.

Figure E-3, one-piece clear glass item with ruffled rim; 6"; collection: Lechler; $60-$75.

Figure E-4, one-piece clear glass item with various types of foliage and animals; 4½"; collection: Mangee; $50-$125.

Figure E-5, Bristol glass with enameled flowers; 6¼"; collection: Lechler; $150-$175.

Figure E-6, contemporary two-piece epergne; frosted thin glass with delicate decoration; collection: Lechler; $75-$100.

Figure E-7, tiny clear glass, two-piece epergne with enameled decorations; rare size; French; 3¾"; collection: Lechler; $200-$300.

Figure E-8, one stem clear epergne with silver base; 3½"; collection: Lechler; $50-$75.

Figure E-9, rare, three-section unit; 4"; collection: Welker; $350-$375.

Figure E-18, one-piece fern and floral; clear with etching; 4½"; collection: Lechler; $50-$125.

Figure E-10, cobalt two-piece epergne; one of a known pair; just under 8"; collection: Lechler; $125-$150.

Figure E-11, light blue transparent glass with heavy white enamel; two-piece; 7¼"; collection: Lechler; $135-$150 each.

Figure E-12, French or Sandwich blue glass with enamel trim; 6¼"; collection: Lechler; $150-$175 each.

Figure E-13, blue transparent glass with enamel; two-piece; 7¼"; collection: Lechler; $135-$170.

Figure E-14, custard glass; no trim; 6"; collection: Mangee; $135-$170.

Figure E-15, light amber, one-piece, very decorative item; looks like an art glass vase on a cake plate; silver base; rare; collection: Welker; $200-$275 each.

Figure E-16, contemporary frosted with blue swirls; collection: Johnston; $75-$100.

Figure E-17, Jackson, blue transparent with opalescent; 6¼"; collection: Mangee; $200-$275.

LUSTERS

Figure LU-1, amethyst glass with deeply ruffled rim and enamel decoration; 6" at shortest point, 7" at tallest point; collection: Lechler; $300-$325 each.

Figure LU-2, pink cased glass with heavy white enamel; about 6½"; collection: Welker; $325-$375.

Figure LU-8, lavender with etching; 6½"; collection: Lechler; $250-$275.

Figure LU-3, cobalt with enameled decoration; 6½"; collection: Lechler; $300-$325 each.

Figure LU-4, grape spattered cased glass; 5¾"; collection: Welker; $275-$375 each.

Figure LU-5, blue spatter cased glass; 5¾"; collection: Lechler; $275-$375 each.

Figure LU-6, pair of pink satin cased glass lusters; 5"; collection: Lechler; $350-$400 each.

Figure LU-7, rare emerald green transparent glass lusters with white enamel; 5¼"; collection: Lechler; $350-$400 each.

MUGS

Most of the mugs in this book are from three collections: Blanche Largent, Joyce Johnston and Jerry and Sandy Schmoker.

†Indicates that a particular mug is shown in color and in a black and white close-up shot.

*Indicates that a mug has been reproduced.

Figure M-1, ROBIN AND NEST: possibly Tarrentum's #352; $50-$75.

†**Figure M-2**, BIRD IN NEST WITH FLOWERS: $50-$60.

Figure M-3, REA: Beatty and Sons; 1½″ x 1¾″, also, 2″ x 3¼″; $18-$22.

†**Figure M-4**, MILL: clear; 2¾″ x 3″; $40-$60.

Figure M-4

†**Figure M-5**, MONKEY with fancy handle: $60-$90.

†**Figure M-2**

†**Figure M-5**

†**Figure M-6**, PLAIN MONKEY: 3⅛″ x 3¼″; $60-$90.

†**Figure M-6**

†**Figure M-12**

Figure M-7, DEER: soda glass shape; unusual; $60-$90.

Figure M-8, LACY DAISY (type) pattern: $20-$40.

Figure M-9, BIRDS AND HARP: 2½″ x 2½″; three sizes in all; McKee Brothers; $40-$60.

Figure M-10, HOBNAIL (type): amber, blue, clear; 2⅜″; $30-$50.

Figure M-11, STIPPLED FORGET-ME-NOT: 2¾″ tall; clear; $50-$90.

†**Figure M-12**, FEEDING DEER: 2⅜″ x 2⅝″; $35-$55.

†**Figure M-13**, LIGHTHOUSE AND SAILBOAT: 2⅛″ x 2⅝″; $40-$60.

Figure M-13

†Figure M-14, WESTWARD HO: 2″; Gillinder and Sons, Greensburg, Pa; $75-$100.

Figure M-15, REA: Beatty and Sons; 1½″ x 1¾″; $15-$20.

Figure M-16, DEER AND COW: 2″; amber, clear, blue, milkglass; $30-$50.

†Figure M-17, LIGHTHOUSE: 2″ x 2½″; $40-$60.

Figure M-18, WEE BRANCHES: 1⅞″; clear, blue; pattern also seen in toy table set, cup, saucer, plate; $40-$60.

Figure M-19, WHIRLING STARS: clear; $10-$12.

Figure M-20, BLOCK No. 1220: also known as Mitered Block; matching toy creamer; $20-$25.

Figure M-21, BEADED candy dip: 1½″; $8-$10.

Figure M-22, STIPPLED ARROWS: Federal Glass Co., catalogue proof shown with rare Grape stein; 1¾″; $25-$40.

Figure M-17

†Figure M-23, CAPTAIN HOOK: 1⅞″; $30-$40.

Figure M-14

Figure M-23

Figure M-24, ST. LOUIS: Westmoreland Specialty Co.; $10-$25.

Figure M-25, THE SANITARY VACUUM BOTTLE CO.: 2⅛"; John B. Higbee; $30-$40.

Figure M-26, DIAMOND BAND: 2¼" x 1¼"; $40-$50.

Figure M-27, HOOK: creamer and matching mug; $22-$28 each.

Figure M-28: clear and possibly color; $25-$40.

Figure M-29: $25-$40.

Figure M-30: amber, clear, blue; $30-$50.

Figure M-31, MIKADO: Richards and Hartley's #99; 1888 catalogue; two mug sizes; clear, amber, blue; $40-$60.

Figure M-32, LEAF AND TRIANGLE: 3⅛" x 3¼"; clear, amber, blue; 2 sizes; $40-$60.

†Figure M-33, DOG CHASING DEER: with beaded handle; Bryce Brothers, Factory B; reissued by U.S. Glass Co., after 1891; part of a beaded handle series which includes: Figure M-56, SWAN; Figure M-61, POINTING DOG; Figure M-81, BIRD ON BRANCH; clear, color, some frosted; $50-$90.

†Figure M-34, BOY WITH BEGGING DOG: 3½" x 3"; $30-$50.

Figure M-35, DEWDROP OR DOT: hobnail style; amber, blue, clear; $40-$60.

Figure M-36, COLORADO, No. 15057: green with hand painting; $50-$75.

Figure M-37, cobalt PANELS: $20-$40.

M-33
Two views

†Figure M-33

139

†Figure M-38, SWAN: with ring handle; clear and color; 2⅜″ x 2⅜″; attributed to Hemingray Glass Co.; $40-$50.

†Figure M-38

Figure M-39, Small DOT: McKee; see ad with Tappan toy table set; $30-$40.

Figure M-40, STIPPLED FORGET-ME-NOT: amber, clear, blue; $50-$80.

Figure M-41, SWIRL: milkglass and clear; $20-$40.

Figure M-42, PANELED CANE: 1¾″ x 2⅜″; clear, cobalt, light blue; $20-$50.

Figure M-43, *DAISY AND BUTTON WITH "V" ornament: also known as VANDYKE; A.J. Beatty and Sons; 2¾″; yellow, amber, blue; reproduced 3 sizes; $30-$50.

Figure M-44: cobalt, milkglass opalescent; $30-$50.

Figure M-45, ORIENTAL: penny candy mug; custard, opaque, green, opaque French blue; Westmoreland Specialty Co.; 1905; $20-$22.

Figure M-46, all over STIPPLED VINE: clear, amber, blue; $40-$60.

Figure M-47, COBALT PENNY CANDY: Federal Glass Co.; $18-$22.

Figure M-48, GRAPE VINE AND OVALS: King Co.; also table set; clear, blue, amber; 3″ x 3″; $40-$60.

Figure M-49: $30-$40.

Figure M-50, GOOSEBERRY: blue milkglass, soft blue, clear; $40-$60.

†Figure M-51, CERES, CAMEO, MEDALLION: 1870; Atterbury and Co.; clear, turquoise, opal, mosaic, amber, dark amethyst; 1⅞″ x 1⅞″; 2½″ x 2⅛″; $60-$80.

Figure M-51

Figure M-52, GRAPE AND FESTOON WITH SHIELD: 1¾" x 2"; 2⅜" x 2½"; clear, color; $40-$60.

Figure M-53, BEADED FRAMES: clear, cobalt, amber; $30-$50.

Figure M-54: $30-$50.

Figure M-55, BEADS IN RELIEF: clear, milkglass, blue opaque; 1¾" x 1¾"; Atterbury and Co.; $40-$60.

Figure M-56, SWAN: with beaded handle; $50-$70.

Figure M-57, CROSS HATCHING: Bryce Brothers; #3812; amber, blue, clear; $30-$50.

†Figure M-58, BY JINGO: 2½"; clear, color; $40-$60.

Figure M-58

Figure M-59: $40-$60.

Figure M-60, KATE GREENAWAY: hand painted milkglass; style; 3⅛"; $40-$60.

Figure M-61, DOG: beaded handle; 2⅞"; Bryce Brothers; shown in rare frosted glass; this is one of the beaded-handle series; $50-$90.

Figure M-62: $50-$70.

Figure M-63, GARFIELD #294: memorial mug; 2"; $125-$200.

†Figure M-64: possibly Sandwich; hand painted; 2¼"; $75-$150.

Figure M-64

†Figure M-65, BEGGING DOG: 2¼″; clear, cobalt; $40-$60.

†Figure M-66, BUTTERFLY AND LOG: 2⅜″ x 2″; $50-$75.

†Figure M-67, SQUIRREL: clear; 2″ x 3″; $40-$60.

†Figure M-68, ABC: Adams and Co; clear, blue milkglass, blue transparent; see also United States Glass Company ad; rare in color; $100-$200.

†Figure M-67

†Figure M-65

Figure M-66

Figure M-68

Figure M-69, RIBBED LEAVES: 2½″ x 2½″; $40-$60.

Figure M-70, NEW YORK HONEYCOMB: clear; flint; applied handle; 2½″ x 2⅞″; $75-$90.

†**Figure M-71**, *BABY ANIMALS: clear and color; 2½″ x 2¾″; reproduced; $40-$50.

†Figure M-72

†*Figure M-71

†**Figure M-72**, CHICKS AND PUGS: clear and color; 1⅞″ x 2″; United States Glass Co.; clear and color; $60-$80.

†**Figure M-73**, CAT-IN-A-TANGLE: clear and color; 2″; $50-$70.

†Figure M-73

143

Figure M-74: $20-$30.

†**Figure M-75**, BUTTERFLY: three sizes; 2″ x 2″; 2½″ x 2¾″; Bryce Higbee; $50-$70.

Figure M-76, ROBIN: 3¼″ x 3½″; 2¼″ x 2¾″; milkglass, blue opaque, amber; $30-$50.

Figure M-77, HERON AND PEACOCK: clear and cobalt; 2¾″ x 2½″; $30-$50.

†Figure M-76

†Figure M-75

Figure M-77

144

Figure M-78, BIRDS AT FOUNTAIN: clear and blue; 1¾″ x 2″; $30-$40.

Figure M-79, STAG AND DEER: clear, cobalt; 2″ Bryce, United States Glass Co.; $40-$60.

Figure M-80, WATERFOWL (Swan): Bryce Brothers, clear, cobalt; 2″ Bryce, United States Glass Co.; $40-$60.

Figure M-79

Figure M-78

Figure M-80

145

Figure M-81

Figure M-81, BIRD-ON-A-BRANCH: 2¾″ x 2¾″; Bryce, United States Glass Co.; $40-$60.

Figure M-82, DOG AND QUAIL: 2¾″ x 3¼″; $50-$65.

Figure M-83, WOLF: clear and color; 3¾″ x 3⅞″; companion mug, RABBIT; $60-$70.

Figure M-83

Figure M-82

Figure M-84, RABBIT: companion mug WOLF; 3¾″ x 3⅞″; $60-$70.

Figure M-85, SCAMPERING LAMB: clear and color; $75-$90.

Figure M-86, STILL RABBIT: companion mug, RUNNING RABBIT #702; also ELEPHANT #728 which is rare and not shown here; Factory C, United States Glass Company; $75-$125.

†Figure M-85

Figure M-84

†Figure M-86

147

†Figure M-87

Figure M-87, *HEISEY'S ELEPHANT: reproduced in colors; rare when old; collection: Largent; $400-$500.

Figure M-88, CAT-IN-A-DRESS AND HAT: clear, milkglass; 2⅜″; rare $70-$100.

Figure M-89, MONKEYS AND VINES: 2½″ x 2½″; $60-$80.

Figure M-88

Figure M-89

Figure M-90, SANTA AND CHIMNEY: Dithridge and Co., Ft. Pitt Glass Works; used a patented process called crystlography on a series of mugs shown in this book; 3″ x 3½″; rare; $100-$150.

Figure M-91, SANTA AND SLEIGH: 3″ x 3½″; Dithridge and Co.; rare; $100-$150.

Figure M-92, LITTLE BO-PEEP: Dithridge and Co.; rare; 3″ x 3½″; $100-$150.

Figure M-91

M-90

Figure M-92

Figure M-93

Figure M-93, LITTLE RED RIDING HOOD: Dithridge and Co.; rare; 3″ x 3½″; $100-$150.

Figure M-94, HMS PINAFORE, LITTLE BUTTERCUP: Dithridge and Co.; 3″ x 3½″; rare; $100-$150.

Figure M-95, FIGHTING CATS: 1⅞″; clear or color; $60-$75.

Figure M-94

Figure M-95

Figure M-96, A GOOD GIRL; A GOOD BOY: 3″ x 3½″; clear or color; reproduced; dark teal has been noted and it appears to be rare and old; $50-$100.

Figure M-96

Figure M-97

Figure M-98, LIBERTY BELL: Adams and Company, 1876; clear or white milkglass; 2″; clear mug, $90-$150; milkglass mug, $200-$300.

Figure M-97, OUR GIRL: 3″ x 3½″; McKee, 1887; clear, color; $40-$75.

Figure M-98

151

Figure M-99

Figure M-99, DRUM: 2½″ x 2¼″; 1⅞″ x 2″; Bryce Higbee, 1880; $50-$60.

Figure M-100: gold trim with drum-like body; $30-$40.

Figure M-101, ALL OVER STARS: 2½″ x 23¼″; $30-$40.

Figure M-100

Figure M-101

152

Figure M-102, HUMPTY-DUMPTY, TOM THUMB: 2¾″ x 3½″; $40-$60.

Figure M-103, LITTLE BO-PEEP: blue or white milkglass, frosted, clear; $40-$60.

Figure M-104, CUPID AND VENUS: clear; Richards and Hartley #500; 2″ x 2½″; 3″; clear, amber, canary; $50-$70.

Figure M-103

Figure M-102

Figure M-104

Figure M-105

Figure M-105, MCKEE'S NEW YORK: 2¼″ x 3½″; $60-$70.

Figure M-106, BANDED STALKS: clear; 2½″ x 2¾″; $30-$50.

Figure M-107, DIVIDED BLOCK WITH SUNBURST: 2¼″ x 3⅜″; $30-$50.

Figure M-106

Figure M-107

154

Figure M-108, STARS AND STRIPES: 2¼″ x 3⅛″; $50-$70.

Figure M-109, RIBBED FORGET-ME-NOT: $40-$70.

Figure M-110, DOYLE #500: amber, clear, blue: $50-$70.

Figure M-109

Figure M-108

PLATE IV

Top Row, left to right

    A. B. C., Adams & Co., Pittsburgh, Pa.
    Saxon, Adams & Co., Pittsburgh, Pa.
    Swan, Bryce Bros., Pittsburgh, Pa.
    Dog, Bryce Bros., Pittsburgh, Pa.
    Bird, Bryce Bros., Pittsburgh, Pa.

Middle Row

    Deer and Dog, Bryce Bros., Pittsburgh, Pa.
    Panelled Daisy, Bryce Bros., Pittsburgh, Pa.
    Rosette, Bryce Bros., Pittsburgh, Pa.
    Fishscale, Bryce Bros., Pittsburgh, Pa.

Bottom Row

    Ribbed Forget-Me-Not, 3 1/4 oz., Bryce Bros., Pittsburgh, Pa.
    Panelled Hobnail, Bryce Bros., Pittsburg, Pa.
    Diamond Waffle, 1 3/4 oz., Bryce Bros., Pittsburgh, Pa.
    Basket Weave, Bryce Bros., Pittsburgh, Pa.
    Looped Panel, Bryce Bros., Pittsburgh, Pa.

PLATE III

Top Row, left to right

    Rabbit, Central Glass Co., Wheeling, W. Va.
    Elephant, Central Glass Co., Wheeling, W. Va.
    Faceted, Small, Doyle & Co., Pittsburgh, Pa.
    Faceted, Medium, Doyle & Co., Pittsburgh, Pa.
    Hobnail, notched handle, 5 3/4 oz., Doyle & Co., Pittsburgh, Pa.

Middle Row

    Hobnail, Thumbprint base, Doyle & Co., Pittsburgh, Pa.
    Pillar and Cut Diamond, Doyle & Co., Pittsburgh, Pa.
    Red Block, Doyle & Co., Pittsburgh, Pa.
    Shell, Doyle & Co., Pittsburgh, Pa.
    Daisy and Button with V-Ornament, Small, A. J. Beatty & Sons, Tiffin, Ohio

Bottom Row

    Daisy and Button with V-Ornament, Medium, A. J. Beatty & Sons, Tiffin, Ohio
    Daisy and Button with V-Ornament, Large, A. J. Beatty & Sons, Tiffin, Ohio
    Daisy and Button with V-Ornament, full-size, A. J. Beatty & Sons, Tiffin, Ohio
    Hobnail, 7 Rows, A. J. Beatty & Sons, Tiffin, Ohio
    Crested Hobnail, cup, 3 oz., A. J. Beatty & Sons, Tiffin, Ohio

PLATE NO. I

Top Row, left to right
Crested Hobnail, etched band, 5 oz., A. J. Beatty & Sons, Tiffin, Ohio
Crested Hobnail, footed, 4½ oz., A. J. Beatty & Sons, Tiffin, Ohio
Mitred Block, A. J. Beatty & Sons, Tiffin, Ohio
Mitred Block, lipped, A. J. Beatty & Sons, Tiffin, Ohio
Spear, A. J. Beatty & Sons, Tiffin, Ohio
Prism, A. J. Beatty & Sons, Tiffin, Ohio

Middle Row
Swirl and Ball, A. J. Beatty & Sons, Tiffin, Ohio
Cut Block and Daisy, Small, Bellaire Goblet Co., Findlay, Ohio
Cut Block and Daisy, Medium, Bellaire Goblet Co., Findlay, Ohio
Cut Block and Daisy, Large, Bellaire Goblet Co., Findlay, Ohio
Cut Block and Daisy, Full size, Bellaire Goblet Co., Findlay, Ohio

Bottom Row
Hobnail, Rope Handle, Bellaire Goblet Co., Findlay, Ohio
Reeded Waffle, Bryce Bros., Pittsburgh, Pa.
Columbia, Columbia Glass Works, Findlay, Ohio
Daisy and Button, scalloped band, Gillinder & Sons, Greensburg, Pa.
Lily-of-the-Valley, Bryce Bros., Pittsburgh, Pa.

PLATE II

Top Row, left to right
Hanover Star, Medium, 5¼ oz., Richards & Hartley, Tarentum, Pa.
Hanover Star, Large, 7¾ oz., Richards & Hartley, Tarentum, Pa.
Three-Panel, Medium, 5¼ oz., Richards & Hartley, Tarentum, Pa.
Three-Panel, Large, 7¾ oz., Richards & Hartley, Tarentum, Pa.
Rustic, Gillinder & Sons, Greensburg, Pa.

Middle Row
Tycoon, Small, 3¾ oz., Columbia Glass Co., Findlay, Ohio
Tycoon, Medium, 5 oz., Columbia Glass Co., Findlay, Ohio
Tycoon, Large, 6½ oz., Columbia Glass Co., Findlay, Ohio
Prism, Cup, Columbia Glass Co., Findlay, Ohio
Crested Hobnail, Tall, Columbia Glass Co., Findlay, Ohio

Bottom Row
Stippled Vine, Small, King Glass Co., Pittsburgh, Pa.
Stippled Vine, Medium, King Glass Co., Pittsburgh, Pa.
Stippled Vine, Large, King Glass Co., Pittsburgh, Pa.
Pressed Oak Leaf, Central Class Co., Wheeling, W. Va.
Cabbage Rose, Central Glass Co., Wheeling, W. Va.

Toys and Mugs.

SCALE FULL SIZE

Small Toy Pillar Mug.

Large Toy Pillar Mug.

Small Dot Mug.

Large Dot Mug.

Hooded Toy Tumbler.

Small Fancy Mug.
(Also make medium and large)

Small New York Mug.
Also make large.

Child's Cup.

No. 80 Mug.
Half Size.

Tappan Spoon.

Tappan Sugar and Cover.

TAPPAN TOY SET.
(HALF SIZE)

Tappan Cream.

Old 4 oz. Ray Mug.
Half Size.

No. 5 4 oz. Ray Mug. Half Size
Also make Sand 8 oz.

Pillar Toy Tumbler.

Gill Toy Tumbler.

Games Toy Tumbler.

Tappan Butter and Cover.

No. 41 Toy Mug.
(Half Size.

No. 6 Toy Mug.
Half Size.

Berry Toy Spoon.

Berry Toy Cream.

158

PLATES
ABC; NUMERAL; NOVELTY

Figure PL-1, INDEPENDENCE HALL: $60-$75.

Figure PL-2, EAGLE: $60-$75.

The maker of these two, 7″ plates is unknown. Information on the plates themselves indicates that they were intended to celebrate the 1876 Centennial Exposition at Philadelphia. Perhaps they were sold on the grounds as souvenirs. Circa 1875-1876. Collection: Johnston.

Figure PL-1
Independence Hall

Figure PL-2
Eagle

Figure PL-3, STORK: $35-$50.

Figure PL-4, LION: $60-$75.

Figure PL-5, DUCKS: $35-$50.

Figure PL-6, RUNNING RABBIT: $35-$50.

Figure PL-7, NIBBLING RABBIT: $60-$75.

The Crystal Glass Company, Pittsburgh, Pennsylvania offered the Stork, Lion and two Rabbit plates to delight the children at Christmas. The source of this attribution is the American Pottery and Glassware Reporter, December 1879. The Duck plate was probably added into the production line in 1880. These plates are 6″ in diameter and were produced between 1879 and 1884. Collections: Stork, Lion, Running Rabbit, Johnston; Ducks, Lubberger; Nibbling Rabbit, Dagenais.

Figure PL-3
Stork

Figure PL-4
Lion

Figure PL-5
Ducks

Figure PL-6
Running Rabbit

Figure PL-7
Nibbling Rabbit

Figure PL-8, HEN AND CHICKS: $50-$75.

Figure PL-9, SITTING DOG: $75-$125.

Figure PL-10, HEN AND CHICKS VARIANT: $50-$75.

The producer of these 6″ plates was King, Son and Company, Pittsburgh. In their catalogues of the 1880s King referred to Hen and Chicks as their "6 inch Toy A.B.C. Plate," and to the Sitting Dog as their "4 inch Toy 1, 2, 3 Plate." Plate No. 10 has a rope-like design circling the rim just below the ABCs which is missing on Plate No. 8. They were advertised along with the Rooster toy table set and have enough pattern similarities to make nice companion pieces. Collections: Sitting Dog, Hen and Chicks Variant, Johnston; Hen and Chicks, Lechler.

Figure PL-8
Hen and Chicks

Figure PL-9
Sitting Dog

Figure PL-10
Hen and Chicks Variant

Figure PL-11, DEER: $35-$50.

Figure PL-12, SANCHO, PANZA AND DAPPLE: $35-$50.

Figure PL-13, FLOWER BOUQUET: $35-$50.

Figure PL-14, FROLIC: $35-$50.

Gillinder and Sons produced these plates and two other larger ones not shown here. One is "Boys in Cart" and the other is "Boys Falling Over Log". Since they are larger, they fall more readily into the bread plate category. The first three plates are 6″ in diameter. All the plates were produced in the 1880s. Collections: Deer, Dagenais; Sancho, Flower, Johnston; Frolic, Largent.

Figure PL-11
Deer

Figure PL-12
Sancho, Panza and Dapple

Figure PL-13
Flower Bouquet

Figure PL-14
Frolic

Figure PL-15, DOG WITH TREE: $35-$50.

Figure PL-16, ELEPHANT: $35-$50.

Figure PL-17, GARFIELD: $50-$65.

Ripley and Company made these three plates with the identical ABC borders. The elephant's howdah has a part of its design "R & Co.", circa 1880-1895. Collections: Dog with Tree, Dagenais; Elephant, Garfield, Johnston.

Figure PL-18, CHRISTMAS MORN: $90-$250.

Figure PL-19, CHRISTMAS EVE: $90-$175.

Figure PL-20, NUMBERS: $90-$125.

These 6″ plates are extremely difficult to find and were probably produced for only a short time. Collections: Christmas Morn, Numbers, Dagenais; Christmas Eve, Johnston.

Figure PL-15
Dog with
Tree

Figure PL-16
Elephant

Figure PL-17
Garfield

Figure PL-18
Christmas Morn

Figure PL-19
Christmas Eve

Figure PL-20
Numbers

Figure PL-21, CLOCK AND NUMBERS CENTER: surrounded by 3-row grid; $25-$35.

Figure PL-22, RAYED AND NUMBERS CENTER: surrounded by 3-row grid; $25-$35.

These are 6″ plates. Collections: Clock and Numbers, Johnston; Rayed and Numbers, Largent.

Figure PL-23, HEX CENTER: $25-$35.

This 6″ plate can be found with an ABC border instead of the motto border. Collection: Lubberger

**Figure PL-23
Hex Center**

**Figure PL-21
Clock and
Numbers Center**

Figure PL-24, BUTTON CENTER: $25-$35.

This is a 6″ plate; Collection: Johnston.

**Figure PL-22
Rayed and
Numbers Center**

**Figure PL-24
Button Center**

Figure PL-25, CLOCK WITH SCALLOPED EDGE: $25-$35.

This 7″ plate was produced by the United States Glass Company, Factory F (Ripley), in the 1890s. Collection: Largent

**Figure PL-25
Clock with
Scalloped Edge**

Figure PL-26, HOBNAIL: $90-$150.

This is a 6″ plate. Collection: Dagenais

**Figure PL-26
Hobnail**

Figure PL-27, CAT: $85-$125.

This 6″ plate was produced by the Columbia Glass Company, Findlay, Ohio. There is a DOG companion plate: $100-$125.

**Figure PL-27
Cat**

*Figure PL-28, LITTLE BO-PEEP: $35-$50.

*Figure PL-29, HEY! DIDDLE DIDDLE: $35-$50.

*Figure PL-30, THIS LITTLE PIG WENT TO MARKET: $35-$50.

Figure PL-31, TEDDY BEARS: $75-$150.

The Indiana Glass Company, Dunkirk, Indiana issued a toy catalogue showing these toy plates, packed 20 dozen to a barrel. All four were offered in crystal or gold. The gold paint was applied to the back of the plate in the style referred to today by collectors as "goofus" glass. Plates are being reproduced today.

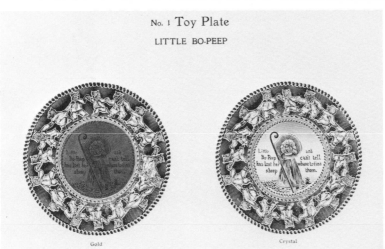

No. 1 Toy Plate

LITTLE BO-PEEP

Gold   Crystal

Figure PL-28

No. 2 Toy Plate

HEY! DIDDLE DIDDLE

Figure PL-29

Gold   Crystal

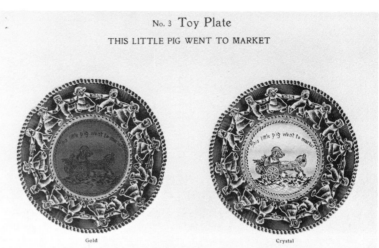

Figure PL-30

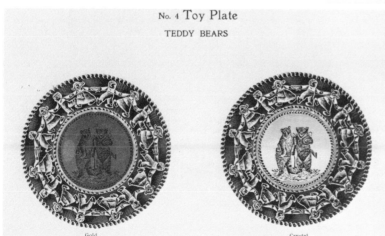

Figure PL-31

Figure PL-65, GOOSE AND RABBITS: milkglass; $60-$80.

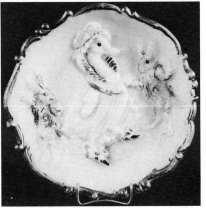

Figure PL-65

Figure PL-66, CHICK IN A SHELL: Lily-of-the-valley-border; clear; $50-$75.

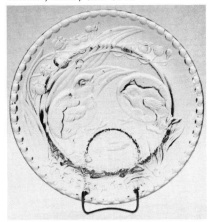

Figure PL-66

Figure PL-67, IOWA CITY MOTTO "BE TRUE": four sizes; four different mottos; 5⅜", also known in 6½"; other sayings: BE PLAYFULL (sic), BE AFFECTIONATE, BE GENTLE; Collection: Lechler; $60-$90.

Figure PL-68, IOWA CITY MOTTO "BE PLAYFULL" (sic): $60-$90.

Figure PL-67

Figure PL-68

166

Figure PL-71, DOG'S HEAD, ABC: New Martinsville #532; blocked off textured alphabet; 6½″; reproduced; $30-$40.

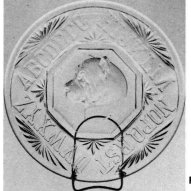

Figure PL-71

Figure PL-72, BOY #531, Emma: clear, blue, amber; alphabet rim; 6½″ diameter; Bryce Higbee; 1893; New Martinsville's #531; reproduced; $35-$40.

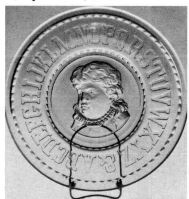

Figure PL-72

Figure PL-9, SITTING DOG: King Glass Co.; numeral border; 4⅛″ diameter; Collection: Lechler, $75-$125.

Figure PL-9

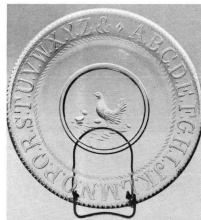

Figure PL-10

167

CAKE AND FRUIT STANDS

Miniature Accessory Plates

Pictured in this section are examples of some of the fruit and cake plates which collectors display with their toy glass.

The Baby Thumbprint pattern offers an open compote and one with a lid, plus two sizes of cake plates. These items are shown in a catalogue reprint as being a part of toy glass history.

The other cake and fruit stands are probably a part of adult glassware lines, but, being small, add balance and interest to a toy glass assemblage.

Figure PL-32

Figure PL-33

Figure PL-34

Figure PL-35

Figure PL-36

Figure PL-37

Figure PL-38

Figure PL-39

Figure PL-40

Figure PL-41

Figure PL-46

Figure PL-44

Figure PL-45

Figure PL-43

Figure PL-47

Figure PL-62

Figure PL-61

Figure PL-56

Figure PL-55

Figure PL-48

Figure PL-49

Figure PL-54

Figure PL-53

Figure PL-51

Figure PL-32, CUPIDS: stemless; 6¾″; Collection: Feltner; $35-$45.

Figure PL-33, CHIMO: 2½″ tall, 6½″ diameter; Collection: Feltner; $30-$40.

Figure PL-34, PERKINS, FORTUNA: 3⅝″; Collection: Mangee; $40-$50.

Figure PL-35, BULLSEYE AND FAN, NO. 15090: 6½″ diameter, 2″ tall; Collection: Feltner; $40-$50.

Figure PL-36, FERN SPRAY: 3⅜″ tall; clear or green; clear, $40-$50.; green, $50-$75.

Figure PL-37, FLORAL OVAL: 3¼″; $40-$50.

Figure PL-38, FROSTED ROMAN KEY: fruit dish, 3½″ tall; Collection: Feltner; $35-$45.

Figure PL-39, LOOPS AND STARS: 3½″; Collection: Feltner; $45-$60.

Figure PL-40, BUTTONS AND LOOPS: 3⅝″; Collection: Mangee; $40-$45.

Figure PL-41, PEAKS AND BUTTONS: 4½″ diameter, 3½″ tall; $40-$50.

Figure PL-35
Bullseye and Fan

Figure PL-41
Peaks and Buttons

171

Figures PL-43-46, TWIN: Twin has multiplied to four different shapes, no doubt using the same mould with various rim shaping; all pieces have a zippered stem, busy design and quality glass.

Figure PL-43, TWIN: cake; 3⅜″ tall and 4¾″ across; Collection: Lechler; $50-$70.

Figure PL-44, TWIN: muffin; 3¾″ tall and 4⅛″ across; Collection: Lechler $50-$70.

Figure PL-45, TWIN: fruit; Collection: Rogers; $50-$85.

Figure PL-46, TWIN: candy; Collection: Rogers; $50-$85.

Figure PL-47, FINE CUT STAR AND FAN: banana stand; 5⅜″ tall and 6⅛″ long; Collection: Feltner; $40-$50.

Figure PL-48, PALM LEAF AND FAN: cake stand: 3¼″ tall, 5¼″ diameter with a turned-up edge; different style cake stand, 4″ tall and 6⅜″ diameter; clear or green; Collection: Feltner; clear, $40-$50; green, $60-$75.

Figure PL-49, PALM LEAF AND FAN: fruit stand; 4¾″ tall, 5¾″ long; Collection: Feltner; $40-$50.

†**Figure PL-51,** BABY THUMBPRINT: covered compote, 3⅞″; around the base is a row of sixteen impressions, the lid has fourteen; Collection: Lechler; $150-$225.

Figure PL-52, BABY THUMBPRINT: flared, open compote; rare; Collection: Lechler; $150-$275.; see page 14.

PL-43 Twin

Figure PL-53, BABY THUMBPRINT: small cake stand, 2″; two rows of bean-shaped impressions; smooth stem; Collection: Feltner; $150-$275. See page 14.

Figure PL-54, BABY THUMBPRINT: larger cake plate; 3″ tall; one row of impressions; paneled stem; Collection: Lechler; $150-$225.

Figure PL-55, BEAUTIFUL LADY: cake plate (2) styles, only one is shown; 3½″ with turned-up rim, 3⅜″ with flat rim; Collection: Feltner; $40-$50.

Figure PL-56, BEAUTIFUL LADY: stemless fruit; 2⅛″ tall, 5⅝″ long; also known with a stem, 5¼″ tall and 6⅝″ long; Collection: Walters; $35-$40.

†**Figure PL-57,** RIBBON CANDY: 3⅜″ tall, 6½″ diameter; clear or green; Collection: Mangee; clear, $50-$60.; green, $75-$80.

Figure PL-54   **Figure PL-53**   **Figure PL-51**

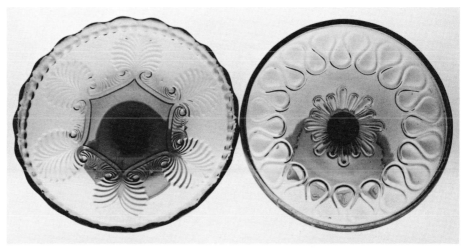

PL-36   PL-57 Ribbon Candy

Figure PL-58, AMERICAN BEAUTY ROSE: 6⅝″ diameter, 3¼″ tall; Collection: Walters; $40-$50.

Figure PL-59, FLOWER WINDOW: 5″ diameter; 2½″ tall; $40-$60.

Figure PL-60, MONK: banana dish, 6½″ long, 4½″ wide; $30-$50.

PL-59 Flower Window

PL-58 American Beauty Rose

PL-60 Monk

Figure PL-61, PARIS, Little Ladders: cake stand; 4″ tall, 6½″ diameter; also known at 3¼″ tall; Collection: Feltner; $45-$60.

Figure PL-62, PARIS, Little Ladders: fruit stand; 5¼″ at the highest point, 6½″ long; Collection: Mangee; $45-$60.

Figure PL-63, LACY DEWDROP: cake stand; also known in 3″ mug; Collection: Feltner; $50-$60.

†**Figure PL-64**, GOOFUS: glass plate with paint; Collection: Feltner; $30-$40.

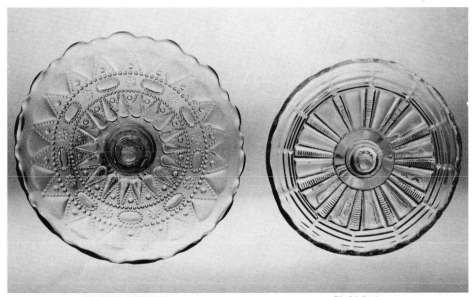

PL-63 Lacy Dewdrop　　　　　　**PL-61 Paris**

SANDWICH GLASS

For more detailed information on toy Sandwich glass, study the publication called: A GUIDE TO SANDWICH GLASS, *Witch Balls, Containers and Toys* by Raymond E. Barlow and Joan E. Kaiser. Most of the items in this section are from the Largent, Feltner and Johnston collections.

Figure SA-1, FINE RIB WITH BAND: toy lemonade tumbler; transparent blue, green, clear, clambroth, ruby, amethyst; 1¾″ x 1⅝″; Collection: Johnston; color is more costly than clear; $35-$40.; clambroth, $80-$90.; ruby, $150-$175.; amethyst, $175-$190.; green, $150-$175.

Figure SA-2, PRESSED PRISM PANEL: 1¾″ x 1¾″; tumbler or mug (both shown); both are considered lemonades; Collection: Johnston; clear, $10-$15.; amber, $100-$150.; blue, $160-$170.; ruby, $150-$175.; amethyst, $150-$160.; green, $160-$175., for either item.

Figure SA-4, LACY TOY FOOTED VEGETABLE DISH: 1⅜″ x 2¾″; Collection: Feltner; $150-$250.

Figure SA-5, TOY OVAL BOWL: scalloped rim; ¾″ tall, 1⅞″ long, 1¼″ wide; Collection: Largent; clear, $50-$75.; clambroth, $150-$160.; opaque white, $275-$300.; amber, $300-$325.; ruby, $400-$450.; amethyst, $450-$475.

†Figure SA-6, PINCH GRIP HANDLE: same pattern with a typical handle shown in figure SA-9; Lacy pitcher shown in this color section has the same grip as pictured in my red book, CHILDREN'S GLASS DISHES, CHINA AND FURNITURE VOL. II, on page, 186. Collection: Feltner; $150-$175.

Figure SA-7, LACY TOY BOWL: low foot; 1″ x 1⅝″; Collection: Feltner; clear, $75-$80; clambroth, $150-$160; opaque white, $275-$290.; amber, $300-$325.; ruby, $400-$450.; amethyst, $450-$500.

Figure SA-8, LACY TOY JUG: 1½″ to 1¾″; Collection: Feltner; clear, $65-$100.; opaque whtie, $250-$275.; ruby, $550-$650.; amethyst, $600-$700.; green $700-$800.

†Figure SA-9, LACY TOY: cup and saucer; cup, 1″ x 1⅛″; saucer, 1⅞″ diameter; Collection: Johnston; clear set, $150-$175.; amber set $400-$500.; ruby set, $600-$800.; amethyst set, $600-$800.

SA-9

---

†indicates an item is shown in color and black and white. Prices are for items in the best possible condition.

Figure SA-10, PRESSED TOY FLAT IRON: ⅞″ tall, 1⅜″ long; Collection: Feltner; clear, $150-$160.; fiery opalescent, $275-$350.; opaque white, $600-$800.; amber, $600-$700.; amethyst, $600-$800.; green, $600-$800.

Figure SA-11, TOY SPOONER HOLDER: 1½″ tall; maker unknown; Collection: Johnston; clear; $30-$35.; color, $35-$45.

Figure SA-12, JUG AND TUMBLER: jug, 2″; tumbler, 1⅛″; clear; Collection: Largent; two pieces, $50-$75.

Figure SA-13, LACY TOY EWER AND BASIN: ewer, 2½″ tall; basin 1″ tall and 3¼″ diameter; Collection: Johnston; prices are for mint or nearly mint sets: clear Lacy, $350-$275.; cobalt blue, $900-$1,200.; ruby, $1,100-$1,500.; amethyst, $1,200-$1,500.

Figure SA-14, CONCENTRIC RINGS: toy lacy plate; 2¼″ diameter; Collection: Johnston; crystal, $75-$100; clambroth, $150-$175.; opaque white, $275-$300; amber, $500-$600; ruby $550-$600; amethyst, $600-$700.; green, $700-$800.

†**Figure SA-15**, BAND OF ROSETTES: toy lacy plate; 2¼″; Collection: Johnston; crystal, $75-$100.; clambroth, $150-$175.; opaque white, $275-$300.; amber, $500-$600.; ruby, $550-$600.; amethyst, $600-$700.; green, $700-$800.

Figure SA-16, LACY OVAL: toy dish; ½″ tall, 3″ long, 2″ wide; Collection: Johnston; cyrstal, $75-$100; clambroth, $150-$175.; opaque white, $225-$275.; amber, $300-$400.; blue, $600-$700.; ruby, $400-$500.; amethyst, $600-$650.

Figure SA-17, TRAY: for tureen; ⅜″ tall, 2¾″ long; 1⅞″

SA-15

wide; pressed Lacy with ferns and scrolls in center with diamonds; Collection: Largent; clear, $100-$150.; opaque white, $200-$250.; amber, $200-$300.; ruby, $250-$300; amethyst, $250-$350.; green, $300-$400.

†**Figure SA-18**, LACY TOY TUREEN: tureen, 1¼″ tall, 3″ long, 1⅞″ wide; lid, ¾″ tall, 2¾″ long, 2″ wide; Collection: Largent; tureen and underplate in each case, complete and mint: clear, $300-$400.; opaque white, $900-$1,200.; orange, $1,500-$2,000.; amber $900-$1,200.; ruby, $1,000-$1,400.; amethyst, $1,200-$1,500.; green, $1,400-$1,800.

SA-18

SA-18

Figure SA-19; SA-20, BLOWN WAFER TRAYS: blue and white 2″ tall, 2½″ diameter; these are so-called wafer trays used to hold wafers for sealing letters; shown here to correct a mistake in a previous book; same in red and white; Collection: Lechler; $300-$400 each.

Figure SA-21, PRESSED PANELED: toy tumbler; 1⅝″; Collection: Johnston; clear, $18-$20; amber, $90-$100; blue, $125-$150.; ruby, $100-$125.; amethyst, $110-$150.; green, $150-$175.

†**Figure SA-22, PRESSED HEXAGONAL**: toy spoon holder; 1¾″ tall, 1½″ diameter; Collection: Feltner; clear, $20-$35.; clambroth, $100-$150.; ruby, $100-$150.; amethyst, $175-$200.; green, $200-$250.

Figure SA-23, PRESSED HEXAGONAL: toy spooner; 1¾″ tall, 1¼″ diameter; Collection: Lechler; clear, $20-$35.; clambroth, $100-$150.; ruby, $100-$150.; green, $200-$300.

Figure SA-24: (same as above in clear)

Figure SA-25: (same as above in blue)

Figure SA-26, PRESSED FLUTE: toy lemonade; 1⅝″ tall, 1⅝″ diameter; Collection: Johnston; clear, $20-$25.; amber, $90-$100.; blue $150-$175.; ruby, $100-$150.; amethyst, $100-$150.; green $175-$200.

Figure SA-27, PRESSED toy plate: 2¾″ diameter; Collection: Johnston; clear, $60-$75.

Figure SA-28, BLOWN MOULDED SUNBURST: toy jug; 2⅛"; 1825-1835; clear; $250-$300.; ruby, $500-$800.

Figure SA-29, PRESSED PANELED: toy sugar bowl; 2" complete; Collection: Schmoker; complete, clear $150-$200.; Complete, amber $500-$600.; complete, ruby $750-$900.; complete, amethyst $850-$1,000.; complete, green $1,000-$1,800.

†**Figure SA-21**: spooner

Figure SA-30, PRESSED PRISM PANEL: toy butter; 1½" tall, complete; clear, $150-$200.

SA-28

SA-29

SA-21

SA-30

Figure Sa-31, PINCH GRIP: cup and saucer; clear, $200-$275.

Figure SA-32, BLOWN MOULDED SUNBURST: toy decanter; wrong stopper is presented; complete with correct stopper the size is 3½″; clear and complete, $450-$550; amber, complete $1,200-$2,000.

SA-31

SA-32

SOWERBY GLASS

John Sowerby Jnr was a talented artist who illustrated children's books. It wasn't long before he was also producing many articles of fancy pressed glass with moulded characters in high relief depicting nursery rhymes. Many of Sowerby's products show designs taken from Walter Crane's *AN ALPHABET OF OLD FRIENDS* which was published in 1874. *THE BABY'S OPERA,* published in 1877 was also a favorite source of character ideas for Sowerby glass.

The trademark of the Sowerby firm was that of a peacock's head which was a fashionable motif of the Aesthetic Movement of the 1880s.

John Sowerby's colorful pressed glass tells of special conditions in the nineteenth century and collectors of today enjoy adding the glass to their toy glass collections.

Sowerby's colors are: flint, a word used to describe a heavy glass containing lead oxide for clear glass products; opaline, an opalescent glass which appears milky by reflected light while showing many blue and golden tints; blanc de lait, a milky version of glass showing sky blue tints in its thinner portions; Queen's ivory, an ivory version of vitro-porcelain which looks a bit like present day milkglass; sorbini, blue and white marbling; rubine, deep red; malachite, green and white marbling.

The Sowerby firm was responsible for the new invention called vitro-porcelain which had the dual qualities of glass and china. This important glass discovery was introduced in 1877. This opaque glass lends itself to many varieties of colors and combinations.

SOWERBY GLASS WORKS
Sowerby & Co., Gateshead-on-Tyne England
Sowerby Ellison Glass Works

Figure SO-1, vitro porcelain, #1293; ORANGES AND LEMONS or London Bridge centerpiece; clear, slag, cream or blue, sapphire, amethyst, black; six piece set; Collection: Lechler; six piece set, $375-$400.

Figure SO-2, vitro-porcelain, #1260, called LAVENDER BLUE; blue, cream and many other colors; Collection: Lechler; $75-$90.

Figure SO-3, #1265, bellows shape, called LITTLE JACK HORNER typical Sowerby color range; Collection: Lechler; $75-$125.

Figure SO-4, #1232; flower spill; called OLD KING COLE; typical Sowerby colors; Collection: Lechler; $60-$90.

Figure SO-5, #1219; posy holder; called BIRDS NEST; typical Sowerby colors; Collection: Lechler; $75-$90.

Figure SO-6, vase; black glass; NURSERY RHYME motif; typical Sowerby colors; Collection: Lechler; $75-$90.

Figure SO-7, posy holder, CINDERELLA; typical Sowerby colors; Collection: Walters; $75-$90.

TOY TABLE SETS

If you have approximately sixty different toy table set patterns in your collection you have nearly every example for this particular four-piece unit which includes a covered butter, a sugar (usually covered), a cream pitcher and a holder for spoons.

Only five out of sixty different patterns have been bothered by reproduction. The Lamb set is the most important of the five patterns to be reissued in colors which are not original. The crystal four piece set is the oldest of this pattern with white milkglass following later, but currently capturing the highest dollar. Strangely enough, the white milkglass creamer and spooner are the most difficult to locate and demand a higher price than the covered pieces in the Lamb pattern. New Lamb has been done in several colors which do not adjust well to the serene style and pattern.

Thumbelina or Flattened Diamond is a pattern which nearly every new collector acquires first. It carries a type of pineapple motif which signals welcome in the home. Though the originals were cast in crystal, this charming set has some pastel, amber and sapphire treatments which are considered to have some age. The covered sugar without handles is thought to be part of the original sets with handles and pastels following a bit later. This particular pattern has been remarketed in a multitude of colors, many of which are quite attractive.

Chimo is an important pattern addition to a toy glass collection. L.E. Smith reproduced the creamer and spooner in crystal and colors.

Hawaiian Lei was originally made in crystal. The old sets have either no bee in the base or a bee with Higbee's HIG placed on the bee's wings and abdomen. Tom Mosser of Cambridge Glass Company has reissued a three piece unit, some in colors, with a bee in the base which excludes the HIG initials.

Tappan was a McKee Glass Company product as shown in an original ad. The unit was reproduced in white milkglass, amethyst, teal green, red and amber by Kemple in the late 1950s and early 1960s.

The rarest toy table set is the Standing Lamb unit. The price for a complete four piece set ranges from $4,000 to $6,000. A few of the more common patterns may be found in the price range from $60 to $100.

Some collectors like to use their toy table sets for special dinner parties with careful guests. Each person might have a different butter dish beside his or her bread plate. A toy spoon holder may hold a tiny bouquet for each of the ladies or cigarettes for a guest's convenience. Each person might have his or her own cream pitcher for coffee or tea while the sugar bowl maintains its original function.

The guide prices in this text are for mint or near mint complete pieces. A price range has been given to accommodate regional differences. Most sets have been priced by the color and piece as well as by the unit.

Measurements will vary because glass making is not exact.

Reproductions will be marked by an *
†indicates a particular set is shown in color and black and white.

Measurements for the table sets were taken as follows:

sugar	—base to finial height
butter	—base to finial height
creamer	—base to pouring spout height
spoon holder	—base to rim height
plate	—diameter
cup or mug	—base to rim height
tray	—diameter

TS-1 Acorn

TS-2 Amazon

183

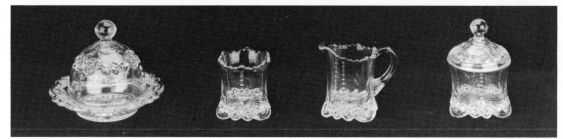

**TS-4
Bead and
Scroll**

**TS-5
Beaded
Swirl**

TS-8 Bucket

TS-11 Buzz Star #15101

184

**TS-14
Cambridge Sweetheart**

**TS-15
Chateau**

TS-16 Chimo

PL-33

185

TS-20
D and M No. 42

TS-23
Drum

M-99

**TS-25
Fine Cut Star and Fan**

**TS-26
Grape
Vine
and
Ovals**

TS-30 Horizontal Threads

TS-32 Liberty Bell

187

188

**Figure TS-39
Oval Star**

**TS-41
Pert**

Rex Pattern

111

Toy Cream
70 dozen in barrel
Gross weight of barrel 190 lbs.

Toy Butter
52 dozen in barrel
Gross weight of barrel 200 lbs.

Toy Spoon
90 dozen in barrel
Gross weight of barrel 190 lbs.

Toy Sugar
60 dozen in barrel
Gross weight of barrel 215 lbs.

**Figure TS-43 Rex
Fancy Cut Tableset**

189

**TS-44
Rooster**

**PL-9
PL-10A
PL-10**

**TS-45
Sawtooth**

See Standing Lamb STORK spooner on page 222.

**TS-46
Standing
Lamb**

TS-50 Style

Figure TS-55
Wabash Series
Tulip and Honeycomb

Figure TS-55

TS-57
Two
Band

TS-58
Wee
Branches

†indicates an item has been shown in color and black and white

*indicates an item has been reproduced

Pattern figure number has been given for the set rather than by the piece.

Pattern names are in alphabetical order.

These close up shots are attempts to show the patterns rather than the shapes of the pieces in the sets.

Figure TS-1, ACORN: Possibly Crystal Glass Company; clear, frosted; rare in clear, very rare in all frosted; not reproduced.

spooner, clear, 3⅛″; $100-$125.
spooner, frosted, $200-$250.
sugar/lid, clear, 4¾″, $150-$350.
sugar/lid, frosted, $200-$350.
creamer, clear, 3⅜″, $100-$125.
creamer, frosted, $200-$350.
butter/lid, clear, 4″, $275-$450.
butter/lid, frosted, $300-$475.
clear set, $700-$800.
frosted set, $800-$1,300.
Collection: Lechler

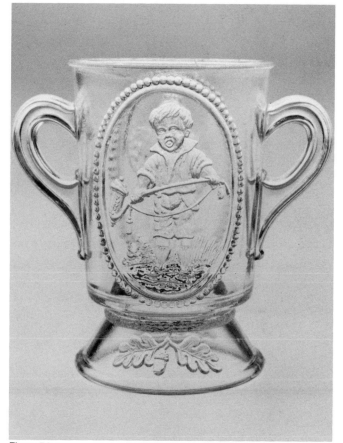

Figure TS-1
Acorn

Figure TS-2, AMAZON, Sawtooth Variation: four piece table set; clear; available; not reproduced.

spooner, 2⅞″, $35-$50.
sugar/lid, 5″, $80-$85.
creamer, 3¾″, $35-$50.
butter/lid, 4¼″, $80-$95.
set, $200-$375.

Collection: Lechler

†**Figure TS-3**, AUSTRIAN No. 200: Greentown; four piece table set; clear, chocolate; rare; not reproduced.

spooner, clear, 2⅞″, $125-$150.
spooner, chocolate, $400-$500.
sugar/lid, clear, 3¾″, $150-$200.
sugar, chocolate, $600-$700.
creamer, clear, 3¼″, $75-$100.
creamer, chocolate, $300-$475.
butter, clear, 2¼″, $225-$300.
butter, chocolate, $800-$900.
set, clear, $500-$750.
set, chocolate, $3,575-$3,800.
Collection: Lechler

Figure TS-2
Amazon

Figure TS-3
Austrian

Figure TS-4, BEAD AND SCROLL: four piece table set; clear, amber, blue olive green, red flashed, gold trimmed, souvenired; available in clear, with gold trim and souvenired; very rare in all colors; not reproduced.

spooner, clear 2½″, $65-$70.
spooner, color, $100-$150.
sugar/lid, clear, 4″, $110-$150.
sugar, color, $150-$200.
creamer, clear, 3″, $65-$70.
creamer, color, $75-$125.
butter, clear, 4″, $150-$200.
butter, color, $225-$400.
set, clear, $375-$550.
set, color, $800-$1,000.
Collection: Lechler

**Figure TS-4
Bead and Scroll**

Figure TS-5, BEADED SWIRL VARIATION: Westmoreland Glass Company; four piece table set; clear, amber, cobalt; common in clear, very rare in color, not reproduced.

spooner, clear, 2⅜″, $40-$50.
spooner, color, $100-$200.
sugar/lid, clear, 3¾″ $40-$45.
sugar/lid, color, $100-$200.
creamer, clear, 2⅝″ $35-$40.
creamer, color, $90-$150.
butter/lid, clear, 2½″, $35-$40.
butter/lid, color, $150-$200.
clear set, $75-$125.
color set, $450-$750.
Collection: Mangee

**Figure TS-5
Beaded Swirl**

†**Figure TS-6** (LARGE) BLOCK, four piece table set; white opalescent, clear, amber, cobalt, blue milkglass; rare; not reproduced.

spooner, clear, 3", $80-$125.
spooner, color, milkglass, $100-$135.
sugar/lid, clear, 4½", $125-$150.
sugar, color, milkglass, $150-$175.
creamer, clear, 3", $60-$75.
creamer, color, milkglass, $75-$100.
butter/lid, clear, 3", $150-$175.
butter, color, milkglass, $160-$200.
set, clear, $375-$400.
set, color, $400-$500.
Collections: Largent; Lechler

**Figure TS-6
Large Block**

†**Figure TS-7**, BRAIDED BELT; four piece table set; hand painted half-flower variations; clear, light green, milkglass with turquoise tint, amber; very rare; prices in this publication reflect any color because it is all rare; not reproduced.

spooner, 2⅝″, $100-$150.
sugar/lid, 3½″, $150-$250.
creamer, 2⅝″, $100-$150.
butter/lid, 2½″, $200-$275.
set, $600-$800.
Collections: Welker; Largent

Figure TS-8, BUCKET, Wooden Pail: Bryce Brothers; four piece table set; clear; very rare; not reproduced.

spooner, 2½″, $200-$250.
sugar/lid, 3¾″, $250-$275.
creamer, 2⅝″, $50-$75.
butter/lid, 2⅜″, $250-$350.
set, $700-$1,000.
Collection: Lechler

Figure TS-7
Braided Belt

Figure TS-8
Bucket

†**Figure TS-60**, BUTTON ARCHES: Duncan Miller Glass Co.; four piece table set, open sugar only; clear, clear with gold or ruby stain; rare; not reproduced.

spooner, $70-$80.
sugar/no lid, 2⅝", $70-$80.
creamer, $50-$70.
butter, 3¾", $150-$170.
set, $400-$475.
Collection: Largent

Figure TS-60
Button
Arches

†**Figure TS-9**, BUTTON PANEL, D and M #44: Duncan and Miller; four piece table set; clear, clear with gold; available; not reproduced.

spooner, 2⅝", $60-$70.
sugar/lid, 4⅝", $80-$90.
creamer, 2⅝", $45-$60.
butter/lid, 4", $100-$125.
set, $275-$375.
Collection: Lechler

Figure TS-9
Button Panel

Figure TS-11, Buzz Star #15101, Whirligig: United States Glass Company; four piece table set, *five to seven piece punch set; clear; green and clambroth spooners known; common in clear; reproduced punch set using incorrect punch bowl mould.

spooner, 2¼″, $30-$40.
sugar/lid, 3⅜″, $30-$40.
creamer, 3⅜″, $30-$40.
butter/lid, 2⅝″, $30-$45.
clear table set, $100-$160.

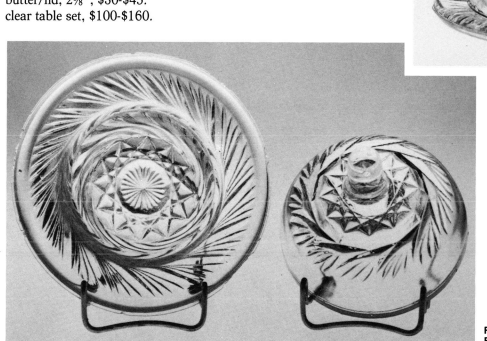

**Figure TS-11
Buzz Star**

199

CAMBRIDGE SERIES as shown in the original ad:

Figure L-0, CAMBRIDGE No. 1: five piece water set; clear, cobalt tumblers; common in clear; not reproduced.

water jug, 3⅛″, $25-$35.
tumbler, 1⅞″, $5-$8.
cobalt tumbler, $12-$25.
set, clear, $50-$75.
Collection: ad

Figure TS-12 CAMBRIDGE COLONIAL No. 2630: four piece table set; clear, cobalt, various shades of green; available; not reproduced.

spooner, clear, 2⅛″, $22-$32.
spooner, color, $30-$38.
sugar/lid, clear, 3″, $28-$32.
sugar, color, $35-$38.
creamer, clear, 2⅜″, $12-$18.
creamer, color, $22-$30.
butter, clear, 2⅛″, $25-$35.
butter, color, $35-$45.
set, clear, $75-$100.
set, color, $125-$175.
Collection: Largent

Cambridge:
Figure L-0: No. 1 water set
Figure TS-12: Colonial table set
Figure TS-13: Fernland table set
Figure TS-10: Buzz Saw table set
Figure P-3: Wheat Sheaf punch set

"NEARCUT" TOY SETS.

Toy Sets are all packed one Complete Set in Paper Cartoon.

ILLUSTRATION FULL SIZE

No. 1 Toy Water Set, 5 Pieces

"Colonial" No. 2630 Toy Tea Set

"Fernland" No. 2635 Toy Tea Set

PRICE LIST.

	List Price Per Doz.	Original Pkg. Doz.
1—Toy Water Set	1 75	14
2630—Toy Tea Set	1 75	6
2635—Toy Tea Set	1 75	6
2697—Toy Tea Set	1 90	6
2660—Toy Punch Set	2 90	7½

We make only the highest grade pot glass.
We make no tank glass.
All quotations made herein are for pot made and not tank.

We quote above prices for FULL PACKAGES ONLY.
When LESS QUANTITY is ordered, ADD 10 PER CENT. to above prices.

No. 2697 Toy Tea Set
Extra Heavy Near Cut

2660 Toy Punch Set—7 Pieces

200

Figure TS-13, CAMBRIDGE FERNLAND No. 2635: four piece table set; clear, cobalt, various shades of green; available; not reproduced.

spooner, clear, 2⅜", ·$28-$32.
spooner, color, $32-$38.
sugar/lid, clear, 3", $32-$38.
sugar, color, $38-$40.
creamer, clear, 2⅜", $28-$32.
creamer, color, $32-$38.
butter/lid, clear, 2¾", $32-$38.
butter, color, $38-$45.
set, clear, $75-$125.
set, color, $125-$175.
Collection: Largent

Figure TS-10, CAMBRIDGE BUZZ SAW No. 2697: four piece table set; clear; common; not reproduced.

spooner, 2⅛", $20-$28.
sugar/lid, 2¼", $30-$38.
creamer, 2½", $20-$28.
butter/lid, 2½", $30-$38.
set, $75-$125.
Collection: Largent

CAMBRIDGE WHEAT SHEAF No. 2660: five to seven piece punch set, five to seven piece berry set, five to seven piece decanter set; clear; all available, but the decanter set is more difficult to locate; not reproduced.

Figure P-3, punch bowl, 3½", $30-$40.
Figure P-3, punch cup, 1¼", $7-$8.50.
Figure B-1, main berry, 2¼", $50-$75.
Figure B-1, small berry, 1", $7-$8.50.
Figure D-19, wine jug, 5¼", $60-$75.
Figure D-19, tumbler, 1¾", $12-$18.
Figure P-3, punch set, $75-$100.
Figure B-1, berry set, $75-$150.
Figure D-19, wine set, $150-$225.
Collections: Johnston; Lechler

CAMBRIDGE INVERTED STRAWBERRY: five to seven piece punch set, five to seven piece (so-called) berry set; clear only, in the old; punch set reproduced by Mosser of Cambridge, Ohio in many colors; old clear punch set is available; berry set is difficult to complete and has not been reproduced to date.

Figure P-1, old punch bowl, 3½", $50-$125.
Figure P-1, old punch cup, 1⅛", $20-$22.
Figure B-3, main berry, 2", $75-$90.
Figure B-3, small berry, 1", $22-$25.
Figure P-1, old punch set, $150-$225.
Figure B-3, berry set, $200-$250.
Collection: Lechler

Figure TS-14, CAMBRIDGE SWEETHEART: four piece table set; clear; common; not reproduced.

spooner, 2″, $18-$22.
sugar/lid, 3″, $18-$22.
creamer, 2⅜″, $10-$15.
butter/lid, 2″, $18-$25.
set, $60-$85.
Collection: Largent

Figure TS-15, CHATEAU No. 714: New Martinsville; four piece table set; five to seven piece punch set; clear; punch set is very rare, table set difficult to complete; not reproduced.

spooner, 2¼″, $40-$40.
sugar/lid, $75-$100.
creamer, 3″, $30-$40.
butter/lid, 4½″ tall, 5¼″ base diameter, $80-$100.
table set complete, $300-$375.
Collection: Mangee

Figure TS-14
Cambridge Sweetheart

Figure TS-15
Chateau

Figure TS-16, CHIMO, Oneata: Riverside Glass Co.; 1908-1909; four piece table set, possible punch set yet unrecorded except for the cup; clear; rare if old; *spooner and creamer reproduced by L.E. Smith.

*spooner, 2⅛", $50-$75.
sugar/lid, 3", $90-$125.
*creamer, 2", $50-$60.
butter/lid, 2⅜", $125-$200.
old table set, $325-$475.
Figure P-13, punch cup, 1½", ⅜" dia., $20-$25.
Figure PL-33, cake plate, 2½" tall; 6½" dia., $40-$60.
Collections: set, Lechler; cake, Feltner

†**Figure TS-17**, CLAMBROTH SCENEY: four piece table set with various scenes, flowers and wording; clambroth, custard glass; rare; not reproduced.

spooner, 2⅜", $100-$150.
sugar/lid, 3¼", $125-$150.
creamer, 2⅝", $75-$80.
butter/lid, 2½", $150-$200.
table set, $475-$600.
Collections: Smith; Lechler

Figure TS-17
Clambroth Scenery

Figure TS-16
Chimo

†**Figure TS-18**, CLEAR AND DIAMOND PANELS: four piece table set with two butter sizes; clear, blue, green; available; not reproduced.

spooner, clear, 2⅜″, $20-$30.
spooner, color, $35-$40.
sugar/lid, clear, 3½″, $30-$40.
sugar, color, $40-$50.
creamer, clear, 2¾″, $15-$20.
creamer, color, $25-$35.
sm. butter, clear, 2⅞″, $30-$40.
sm. butter, color, $40-$50.
lg. butter, clear, 4″, $75-$80.
lg. butter, color, $125-$160.
clear set/two butters, $100-$200.
color set/two butters, $175-$300.
Collection: Lechler

†**Figure TS-19**, CLOUD BAND: Gillinder; four piece table set; clear, white milkglass, with hand painting; rare; not reproduced.

spooner, 2⅜″, $75-$100.
sugar/lid, 4″, $125-$150.
creamer, 2½″, $75-$100.
butter/lid, 3¾″, $150-$200.
set, $425-$600.
Collection: Lechler

Figure TS-19
Cloud Band

Figure TS-18
Clear and
Diamond Panels

Figure TS-20, D and M No. 42, Mardi Gras: Duncan and Miller Company; four to five piece table set, rose bowl; clear, clear with gold, clear with red flashing; scarce with the butter being difficult to find; not reproduced.

spooner, 2¾″, $55-$60.
sugar/lid, 4½″, $75-$125.
fat creamer, 2⅞″, $85-$100.
butter/lid, 4¼″, $200-$325.
honey jug, 2⅜″, $55-$65.
rose bowl, 2⅛″, $75-$100.
five piece table set, $500-$600.
Collection: Lechler

†**Figure TS-21**, DEWDROP, DOT: Columbia Glass Company; four piece table set; clear, amber, blue; rare; not reproduced.

spooner, clear, 2⅝″, $50-$60.
spooner, color, $65-$75.
sugar/lid, clear, 4″, $80-$100.
sugar, color, $100-$125.
creamer, clear, 3″, $50-$60.
creamer, color, $65-$75.
butter, clear, 2⅝″, $150-$160.
butter, color, $160-$185.
clear set, $350-$400.
color set, $400-$450.
Collection: Lechler

Figure TS-20
D and M #42

Figure TS-21
Dewdrop, Dot

†**Figure TS-22**, DOYLE #500: Doyle and Company; five piece table set, mugs; clear, amber, blue, canary; very rare in canary, other shades available; not reproduced.

spooner, clear, 2⅜″, $50-$60.
spooner, color, $65-$75.
sugar/lid, clear, 3⅝″, $65-$75.
sugar, color, $75-$125.
creamer, clear, 2½″, $45-$50.
creamer, color, $55-$75.
butter/lid, clear, 2¼″, $75-$125.
butter, color, $125-$160.
tray, 6⅝″, $100-$125.
clear five-piece set, $225-$325.
color five-piece set, $350-$400.

canary five-piece set, $400-$500.
Figure M-110, mugs, 2″, $40-$60.
Collections: Lechler; canary pieces: Largent

Figure TS-23, DRUM: four piece table set, mugs; clear; available; not reproduced.

spooner, 2⅝″, $65-$85.
sugar/lid, 3¼″, $150-$175.
creamer, 2¾″, $60-$75.
butter/lid, 2¼″, $125-$175.
Figure M-99, mugs, 2″, 2½″, *2³⁄₁₆″, $50-$75.
table set, $400-$575.
Collections: set, Lechler; mugs, Johnston

Figure TS-22
Doyle #500

Figure TS-23
Drum

206

Figure TS-24, EUCLID, Rexford: Higbee Company; four piece table set; clear; not reproduced.

spooner, 2¼″, $35-$45.
sugar/lid, 2¾″, $35-$45.
creamer, 3¼″, $25-$30.
butter/lid, 2⅝″, $35-$45.
set, $95-$150.
Collection: Mangee

Figure TS-25, FINE CUT STAR AND FAN, Ten-Point Star: Higbee; four piece table set; clear; available; not reproduced.

spooner, 2¼″, $30-$40.
sugar, 3⅛″, $30-$40.
creamer, 2⅜″, $22-$25.
butter/lid, 2¾″, $30-$40.
set, $100-$150.

Figure TS-24
Euclid

Figure TS-25
Fine Cut Star and Fan

Figure TS-26, GRAPE VINE WITH OVALS: McKee; four piece table set; complete only in clear; amber, blue creamers only; available; not reproduced.

spooner, 2″, $60-$75.
sugar/lid, 2⅞″, $75-$100.
creamer, 2⅛″, $50-$60.
butter/lid, 1¾″, $85-$125.
clear set, $300-$400.
colored creamers (only), $25-$40. each
Collection: Lechler

*Figure TS-27, HAWAIIAN LEI: Higbee Company, four piece table set; only clear set made originally; common; heavily reproduced in many colors.

spooner, 2¼″, $30-$40.
*sugar, 3″, $30-$35.
*creamer, 2¾″, $25-$30.
*butter/lid, 2¼″, $35-$45.
Figure PL-70, cake plate, 3½″ tall, 6⅝″ dia., $45-$60.
old set, $60-$150.
Collection: Johnston

Figure TS-27
Hawaiian Lei

Figure TS-26
Grape Vine with Ovals

Figure PL-70

†**Figure TS-28, HEISEY'S SAWTOOTH BAND No. 1225:**
four piece table set; clear, clear with gold, clear with ruby
flashing; scarce; take care in getting the correct sugar base,
the custard cup is a bit like the sugar base; not reproduced.

spooner, 2½″, $60-$100.
sugar/lid, 4⅛″, $100-$155.
creamer, 2¾″, $50-$100.
butter/lid, 4″, $150-$175.
set, $350-$550.
Collection: Lechler

Figure TS-28
Heisey's Sawtooth Band

†**Figure TS-29, HOBNAIL WITH THUMBPRINT BASE**
No. 150: Doyle and Company; five piece table set; clear,
amber, blue; available; not reproduced.

spooner, clear, 2⅞″, $45-$50.
spooner, color, $75-$85.
sugar/lid, clear, 4″, $60-$75.
sugar/lid, color, $100-$125.
creamer, clear, 3⅜″, $40-$60.
creamer, color, $60-$70.
butter/lid, clear, 2″, $60-$75.
butter/lid, color, $75-$125.
tray, 7⅜″, $50-$100.
clear five piece set, $300-$375.
color five piece set, $375-$475.
Collection: Lechler

Figure TS-29
Hobnail/Thumbprint Base

Figure TS-30, HORIZONTAL THREADS: four piece table set; clear, cobalt, clear with red flashing; scarce; not reproduced.

spooner, 2⅛″, $40-$50.
sugar/lid, 3⅜″, $50-$75.
creamer, 2¼″, $40-$50.
butter/lid, 2″, $75-$125.
clear set, $175-$225.
red flashed set, $200-$300.
Collection: Lechler

Figure TS-30
Horizontal Threads

†*Figure TS-31, LAMB: four piece table set; old in clear, white milkglass, or white doeskin; scarce in old; *heavily reproduced butter, sugar, creamer in carnival colors and white milkglass.

spooner, clear, 2¾″, $100-$150.
spooner, old milkglass, $200-$250.
sugar/lid, clear, 4⅜″, $125-$175.
sugar, old milkglass, $175-$250.
creamer, clear, 2⅞″, $80-$100.
creamer, old milkglass, $200-$250.
butter/lid, clear, 3⅛″, $175-$200.
butter/lid, old milkglass, $175-$200.
old clear set, $400-$650.
old milkglass or doeskin, $600-$800.
Collection: Lechler

Figure TS-31
Lamb

Figure TS-32, LIBERTY BELL: Adams and Co.; four piece table set, mug; clear table set; a white milkglass creamer has been recorded; clear or milkglass mugs; scarce; not reproduced.

spooner, 2⅜″, $300-$400.
sugar/lid, 3⅝″, $135-$165.
creamer, clear, 2½″, $85-$125.
creamer, milkglass, $150-$300.
butter/lid, 2¼″, $200-$275.
clear set, $650-$800.
Figure M-98, mug, clear, 1⅞″, $90-$150.
Figure M-98, mug, milkglass, $200-$300.
Collections: mug, Johnston; table set, Lechler

**Figure TS-32
Liberty Bell**

Figure TS-33, LION: four piece table set, cup and saucer; clear, frosted, clear with frosted heads; available; not reproduced, but some people have been known to frost the pieces to make them more desirable.

spooner, clear, 3⅛″, $60-$75.
spooner, frosted, $100-$125.
spooner, frosted head, $125-$150.
sugar/lid, clear, 4⅝″, $100-$125.
sugar/lid, frosted, $110-$150.
sugar/lid, frosted head, $150-$175.

**Figure TS-33
Lion**

211

creamer, clear, 3⅜″, $50-$75.
creamer, frosted, $60-$80.
creamer, frosted head, $100-$125.
butter/lid, clear, 2¾″, $125-$150.
butter/lid, frosted, $150-$160.
butter/lid, frosted head, $200-$225.
Figure CUP-12, cup/saucer, clear, $50-$60.
Figure CUP-12, cup/saucer, frosted, $65-$75.
Figure CUP-12, cup/saucer, frosted head, $75-$100.
clear table set, $325-$400.
frosted table set, $500-$600.
frosted heads table set, $550-$650.
Collection: Lechler

Figure TS-34, LONG DIAMOND: correct name POINTED JEWEL; Factory J of United States Glass Company, four piece table set; clear; rare; not reproduced.

spooner, 2½″, $100-$125.
sugar/lid, 3⅞″, $125-$175.
creamer, 2⅞″, $75-$100.
butter/lid, 2″, (1″ base ht., 3⅛″ across base rim) $175-$200.
set, $450-$600.
Collection: Lechler

**Figure TS-34
Long Diamond**

†**Figure TS-35**, MENAGERIE: Bryce Higbee; four piece table set; clear, amber, blue; complete turtle, very rare; bear with no slot, rare; other piece available; not reproduced.

fish spooner, clear, 2⅜″, $75-$150.
fish, color, $150-$175.
bear, sugar, clear/slot, 4¼″, $75-$150.
bear, clear, no slot, $200-$225.
bear, color/slot, $225-$250.
bear, color, no slot, $350-$375.
owl, creamer, clear, 3¾″, $75-$100.
owl, color, $150-$175.
turtle/lid, butter, clear, 2⅜″, $1,000-$2,000.
turtle/lid, color, $2,000-$2,500.
clear set, $2,000-$3,000.
color set, $3,000-$3,800.
Collection: Lechler

†**Figure TS-35**
Menagerie

†Figure TS-35
Menagerie

†Figure TS-35
Menagerie

214

†**Figure TS-36**, MICHIGAN No. 15077, Loop and Pillar: four piece table set, five to seven piece water set, nappy, five to seven piece stein set; clear, sunrise, gold decorated, red and green trim; available in clear or clear with gold; rarest in all over red with gold trim; scarce with red and green trim; not reproduced.

spooner, clear or clear/gold, 3″, $30-$50.
spooner, red/green, $50-$75.
spooner, all red/gold, $200-$275.
sugar/lid, clear or clear/gold, $50-$75.
sugar/lid, red/green, 4¾″, $75-$100.
sugar/lid, all red/gold, $250-$300.
creamer, clear, 2⅞″, $30-$40.
creamer, red/green, $45-$85.
creamer, all red/gold, $100-$125.
butter/lid, clear/gold, 3¾″, $75-$125.
butter/lid, red/green, $125-$175.
butter/lid, all red/gold, $250-$350.
clear table set, $225-$300.
red/green table set, $300-$450.
all red/gold table set, $900-$1,200.
Collections: all red/gold, Largent; other, Lechler

†**Figure TS-36**
Michigan

†**Figure TS-37, NORTHWOOD HOBNAIL:** four piece table set; white opalescent; very rare in completion; not reproduced.

spooner, 2⅞″, $100-$150.
sugar/lid, 3¾″, $200-$225.
creamer, 3″, $50-$75.
butter/lid, 2⅝″, $250-$325.
3¾″ lid diameter
3¹⁵⁄₁₆″ base diameter
set, $475-$675.
Collection: private

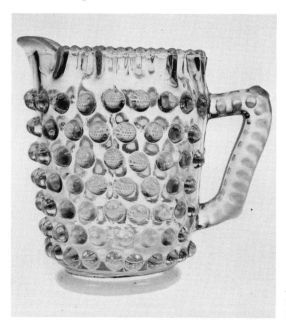

†Figure TS-37
Northwood
Hobnail

†**Figure TS-38, NURSERY RHYME:** four piece table set, five to seven piece water set, five to seven piece berry set, five to seven piece punch set; table set in clear only; available; not reproduced.

spooner, 2½″, $70-$100.
sugar/lid, 4″, $70-$100.
creamer, 2½″, $50-$60.
butter/lid, 2⅝″, $75-$100.
table set, $250-$300.
Collection: Lechler

Figure TS-38
Nursery Rhyme

Figure TS-39, OVAL STAR No. 300: Indiana Glass Company; four piece table set, five to seven piece water set, five to seven piece punch set, five to seven piece berry set; clear with or without gold; table set is common; not reproduced.

spooner, 2½″, $30-$40.
sugar/lid, 4¼″, $22-$32.
creamer, 2⅝″, $18-$20.
butter/lid, 3½″, $25-$30.
table set, $75-$125.
Collection: Lechler

†**Figure TS-40, PENNSYLVANIA No. 15048:** United States Glass Company; four piece table set; clear with or without gold, green with or without gold; available in clear, rare in green and green with good gold; not reproduced.

spooner, clear, 2½″, $40-$50.
spooner, color, $125-$140.
sugar/lid, clear, 4″, $75-$90.
sugar/lid, color, $200-$250.
creamer, clear, 2½″, $40-$50.
creamer, color, $75-$125.
butter/lid, clear, 3½″, $100-$125.
butter/lid, color, $225-$250.
crystal set, $225-$300.
color set, $600-$800.
Collection: Lechler

Figure TS-39
Oval Star No. 300

Figure TS-40
Pennsylvania

Figure TS-41, PERT: four piece table set; clear; available; not reproduced.

spooner, 3½", $75-$100.
sugar/lid, 5⅛", $75-$100.
creamer, 3⅝", $65-$75.
butter/lid, 2⅞", $100-$125.
set, $275-$400.
Collection: Lechler

†**Figure TS-42**, PLAIN PATTERN No. 13: FROSTED RIBBON DOUBLE BAR; King Glass Company; four piece table set; clear, clear with frosted ribbons, cobalt, white opalescent milkglass; scarce in clear, very rare with any variation or color; not reproduced.

spooner, clear, 2¼", $75-$100.
spooner, color or milkglass, $125-$175.
sugar/lid, clear, 3⅜", $125-$185.
sugar/lid, color or milkglass, $200-$275.
creamer, clear, 2½", $60-$75.
creamer, color or milkglass, $100-$150.
butter/lid, clear, 2⅛$100-, $135-$160.
butter/lid, color or milkglass, $225-$300.
clear set, $400-$500; frosted ribbon set, $600-$700.
color or milkglass set, $500-$750.
Collection: Lechler

Figure TS-41
Pert

†**Figure TS-42**
Plain Pattern #13

218

Figure TS-43, REX, Fancy Cut: Co-Operative Flint Glass Company; four piece table set; five to seven piece lemonade set; five to seven piece punch set; clear with or without gold; blue pieces have been seen; table set is available; not reproduced.

spooner, 2¼″, $35-$45.
sugar/lid, 3⅛″, $35-$50.
creamer, 2¼″, $30-$35.
butter/lid, 2⅜″, $40-$50.

clear table set, $125-$150.
color set, $400-$600.
Collection: Mangee

Rex Pattern

Toy Cream
70 dozen in barrel
Gross weight of barrel 190 lbs.

Toy Butter
52 dozen in barrel
Gross weight of barrel 200 lbs.

Toy Spoon
90 dozen in barrel
Gross weight of barrel 190 lbs.

Toy Sugar
60 dozen in barrel
Gross weight of barrel 215 lbs.

Toy Punch Bowl
10 dozen in barrel

Toy Custard
150 dozen in barrel

11 in. Banquet
1 dozen in barrel

Toy Tumbler
200 dozen in barrel

Toy Tankard
30 dozen in barrel

111

**Figure TS-43
Rex**

Figure TS-44, ROOSTER No. 140: King Glass Company; four piece table set, nappy, plates with two different designs; table set is rare, nappy is very rare; not reproduced.

spooner, 3⅛″, $175-$200.
sugar/lid, 4½″, $200-$300.

creamer, 3⅜″, $150-$175.
butter/lid, 3¼″, $250-$325.
nappy, Figure PL-10A, 3″ across, $150-$200.
plate, Figure PL-10, 6″, $60-$75.
table set, Figure TS-44, $650-$950.
Collections: nappy, Feltner; other, Lechler

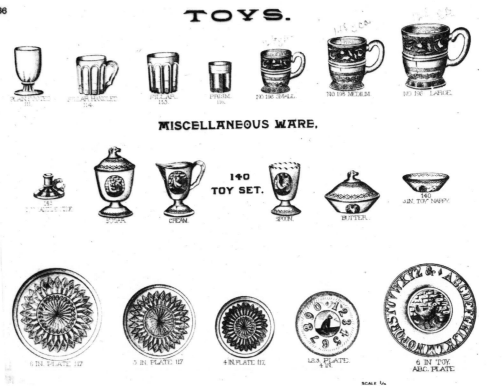

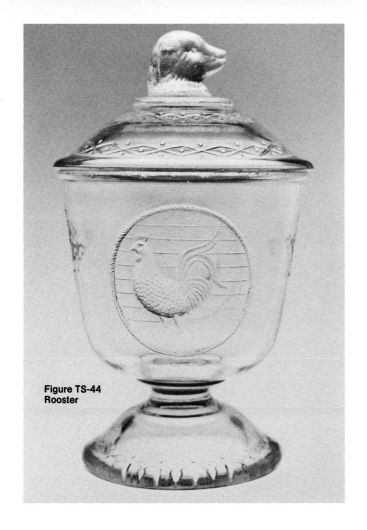

**Figure TS-44
Rooster**

Figure TS-45, SAWTOOTH: four piece table set; clear; available; not reproduced.

spooner, 3⅛", $40-$48.
sugar/lid, 5", $40-$60.
creamer, 3½", $30-$50.
butter/lid, 3", $40-$60.
set, $125-$260.
Collection: Johnston

**Figure TS-45
Sawtooth**

Figure TS-46, STANDING LAMB: may be from Crystal Glass Company; four piece table set; clear, frosted; this is the rarest set in toy glass collections of today; not reproduced; set features: STORK holding the bowl spooner; dog holding the bowl sugar with a cat lid finial; snake-handled creamer; standing lamb butter finial.

spooner, 3½" ht., 2⅛" across rim, $1,200-$1,500.
sugar/lid, 5⅛", $900-$1,000.
creamer, 3¼", $900-$1,200.
butter/lid, 3¾", $900-$1,000.
set, clear or frosted, $4,000-$6,000.
Collection: Lechler

**Figure TS-46
Standing Lamb**

222

†**Figure TS-47**, STIPPLED DIAMOND; STIPPLED FORGET-ME-NOT: four piece table set, mug; clear, amber, blue; rare in clear, very rare in color; no complete set is known to date in Stippled Forget-Me-Not in clear or color; not reproduced. (Detailed prices here are for Stippled Diamond. Prices for Stippled Forget-Me-Not would be double in clear or color.)

spooner, clear, 2⅛″, $70-$85.
spooner, color, $100-$125.
sugar/lid, clear, 3⅛″, $100-$125.
sugar, color, $150-$175.
creamer, clear, 2¼″, $70-$80.
creamer, color, $100-$125.
butter/lid, clear, 2¼″, $125-$150.
butter, color, $160-$175.
Stippled Diamond mug, $40-$60.
Stippled Forget-Me-Not mug, Figures M-11; M-40, $50-$75.
clear table set, $425-$485.
color table set, $600-$700.
Collections: mug, Largent; table set, Lechler

Figure TS-47
Stippled Diamond

†**Figure TS-48**, STIPPLED RAINDROP AND DEWDROP: four piece table set; clear, amber, blue; rare in clear, very rare in color; not reproduced.

spooner, clear, 2⅛″, $60-$75.
spooner, color, $100-$125.
sugar/lid, clear, 3⅛″, $85-$125.
sugar/lid, color, $150-$175.
creamer, clear, 2¼″, $70-$80.
creamer, color, $100-$125.
butter/lid, clear, 2″, $100-$150.
butter/lid, color, $150-$175.
clear set, $350-$425.
color set, $600-$750.
Collection: Lechler

Figure TS-48
Stippled Raindrop
and Dewdrop

†**Figure TS-49, STIPPLED VINE AND BEADS:** four piece table set; clear, amber, blue, teal; scarce in clear, very rare in color; not reproduced.

spooner, clear, 2⅛", $60-$75.
spooner, color, $100-$125.
sugar/lid, clear, 3⅛", $100-$125.
sugar/lid, color, $150-$175.
creamer, clear, 2½", $60-$75.
creamer, color, $130-$160.
butter/lid, clear, 2½", $125-$140.
butter/lid, color, $150-$175.
clear set, $350-$400.
color set, $550-$750.
Collection: Lechler

Figure TS-50, STYLE, Madora, Arrow-Head-In-Ovals: Higbee, 1908-1918; four piece table set, cake stand in miniature; clear; common; not reproduced.

spooner, 2¼", $30-$35.
sugar/lid, 3⅛", $30-$35.
creamer, 2⅜", $22-$25.
butter/lid, 2½", $30-$45.
miniature cake stand, 3¼" tall, 6¼" dia., $40-$50.
set, $90-$135.
Collection: Mangee

†Figure TS-49
Stippled Vine and Beads

Figure TS-50
Style

†**Figure TS-51**, Sultan: McKee Glass Company; four piece table set; clear, green, green frosted, chocolate; rare in green or green frosted and chocolate; not reproduced; Fenton Art Glass Company now owns these moulds.

spooner, crystal, 2½″, $75-$100.
spooner, green transparent, $100-$125.
spooner, green frosted, $150-$175.
spooner, chocolate, $350-$400.
sugar/lid, clear, 4½″, $125-$150.
sugar, green transparent, $150-$175.
sugar, green frosted $200-$275.
sugar, chocolate, $500-$600.
creamer, clear, 2½″, $50-$65.
creamer, green transparent, $100-$125.
creamer, green frosted, $150-$175.
creamer, chocolate, $350-$400.
butter/lid, clear, 3¾″, $125-$175.
butter, green transparent, $250-$275.
butter, green frosted, $350-$375.
butter, chocolate, $600-$675.
crystal set or crystal frosted with or without paint, $400-$475.
green transparent set, $500-$650.
green frosted set, $600-$750.
chocolate set, $2,200-$2,700.
Collections: Lechler; green frosted butter, Largent

Figure TS-51
Sultan

Figure TS-52, SUNBEAM No. 15139: Twin Snowshoes; Gas City, Indiana; McKee; 1894-1908; four piece table set; clear; rare; not reproduced.

spooner, 2¼", $100-$175.
sugar/lid, 3⅛", $150-$225.
creamer, 2¾", $75-$85.
butter, 2", $150-$200.
set, $450-$600.
Collection: Lechler

†*Figure TS-53, TAPPAN:** McKee Glass Company; four piece table set; clear; reproduced in milkglass, cobalt, black, amethyst, green, honey, amber, aqua, old Virginia blue, West Virginia red during the 1950s and 1960s by Kemple; clear is common, color is more collectible.

spooner, clear, 2⅝", $20-$35.
sugar/lid, clear, 4", $25-$35.
sugar/lid, color, $40-$50.
creamer, clear, 2⅞", $20-$25.
creamer, color, $30-$40.
butter/lid, clear, 3⅛", $30-$35.
butter/lid, color, $40-$50.
clear set, $75-$125.
color set, $150-$250.
Collection: Largent

Figure TS-52
Sunbeam, Twin Snowshoes

†*Figure TS-53
Tappan

†*Figure TS-54, THUMBLEINA, Flattened Diamond: four piece table set, five to seven piece punch set; clear, color; heavily reproduced in color.

spooner, clear, 2¼", $20-$30.
spooner, old color, $40-$50.
sugar/lid, clear, 2¼", $20-$35.
sugar, old color, $45-$55.
creamer, clear, 2⅜", $18-$20.
creamer, old color, $35-$45.
butter/lid, clear, 2½", $30-$38.
butter/lid, old color, $50-$65.
clear set, $75-$100.
old color set, $175-$275.
Collection: Largent

**†*Figure TS-54
Thumbleina,
Flattened Diamond**

Figure TS-55, TULIP AND HONEYCOMB: Wabash series; Federal Glass Company, Columbus, Ohio; four piece table set plus an extra butter; four piece vegetable serving set; five to seven piece punch set; clear; table set and punch set, common; vegetable set and small butter are scarce; not reproduced.

spooner, 2½", $20-$30.
sugar/lid, 3¾", $30-$40.
creamer, 2⅝", $20-$25.
small butter, 2⅛", $60-$80.
large butter, 3¼", $38-$45.
table set/ two butters, $150-$200.
Figure TS-55A, open oval bowl, 1¾", $75-$90.
Figure TS-55A, open round bowl, 1¾", $75-$90.
Figure TS-55A, oval covered dish, 2½", $75-$90.
Figure TS-55A, round covered dish, 3⅝", $75-$90.
Figure TS-55A, vegetable set, $375-$400.
Collections: Haskell; Lechler

Figure TS-55A
Vegetable Set

†**Figure TS-56**, TWIST No. 137: Albany Glass Company; four piece table set with butter lid and sugar lid interchangeable; crystal, white, yellow, blue opalescent, frosted, frosted with colored rim rings; rare in opalescent and frosted with color, common in clear; not reproduced.

spooner, clear, 2½″, $25-$35.
spooner, frosted, $40-$50.
spooner, frosted/color, $75-$125.
spooner, opalescent, $200-$250.
sugar/lid, clear, 3⅞″, $25-$35.

sugar, frosted, $60-$100.
sugar, frosted/color, $100-$150.
sugar, opalescent, $200-$250.
creamer, clear, 2⅞″, $20-$28.
creamer, frosted, $40-$50.
creamer, frosted/color, $75-$125.
creamer, opalescent, $200-$250.
butter/lid, clear, 2½″, $25-$35.
butter, frosted, $60-$100.
butter, frosted/color, $100-$200.
butter, opalescent, $200-$250.
clear set, $100-$125.
frosted set, $250-$300.
frosted/color set, $400-$600.
opalescent set, $700-$800.
Collection: Lechler

†**Figure TS-56**
Twist No. 137

228

Figure TS-57, TWO BAND: LaBelle Glass Co; four piece table set; clear; available; not reproduced.

spooner, 2¾", $40-$70.

sugar/lid, 3⅞", $50-$80.

creamer, 2¾", $40-$60.

butter/lid, 2", $60-$100.

set, $250-$350.

Collection: Johnston

**Figure TS-57
Two Band**

Figure TS-58, WEE BRANCHES: clear four piece table set, cup and saucer, plate, mug; mugs, white or blue milkglass, opaque soft blue, cobalt, crystal; table set cup, saucer and plate are rare; not reproduced.

spooner, 2⅜", $75-$85.

sugar/lid, 3", $125-$150.

creamer, 2¼", $75-$85.

butter/lid, 2", $150-$175.

table set, $425-$550.

Figure PL-73, plate, 2½", $60-$75.

Figure CUP-13, cup, 1¾" ht., 2⅜" dia., saucer, 3"

Figure CUP-13, cup and saucer set, $50-$75.

Figure M-18, mug, 1⅞" x 2" $40-$60.

Collection: Lechler

**Figure TS-58
Wee Branches**

†**Figure** TS-59, WILD ROSE: four piece table set, (P-12) five to seven piece punch set, candlestick; table set in white milkglass, punch set in white milkglass and crystal; clear punch set and clear candlestick (C-35) are rare; other items are available; not reproduced.

spooner, 1⅞″, $30-$40.
open sugar, 1⅞″, $50-$60.
creamer, 2″, $50-$60.
butter, 3⅞″, $65-$85.
table set, $190-$250.

†**Figure TS-59**
Wild Rose

Typical Toy Glass Ad from a Butler Brothers Catalogue.

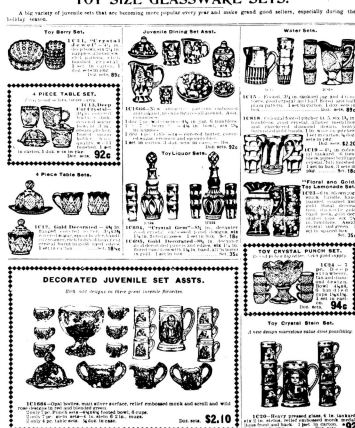

MISCELLANEOUS

Figure M-1: SISTERS; rose bowls; two sizes available; etched children on clear glass; also called Two Sunbonnet Girls from *THREE LITTLE GIRLS WERE SITTING ON A RAIL;* Collection: Lechler; either size, $75-$150.

Figure M-2: rose bowl; 2″ tall; clear; Collection: Mangee; $40-$60.

Figure M-3: tea sandwich plate; possibly Cambridge; Collection: Haskell; $30-$38.

Figure M-4: swirled table pieces; covered cheese, creamer, covered dishes of various sizes; age unknown; Collection: Largent, priced by the piece, $18-$25.

Figure M-5: ice cream cone holders; 2⅝″ tall, 2⅝″ across base, 1¼″ across top; plain rim holder, 2½″ tall; some with a chain of hearts on base; Collection: Lechler; $60-$70.

Figure M-6: art glass miniature basket in holder; Collection: Neale; $150-$200.

Figure M-7: vase; blue Bristol glass with hand painted flowers; Collection: Lechler; $40-$75.

Figure M-8: French swirl goblets; usually found with decanters in French china (boxed-set) of dishes; known colors are green, blue and clear; not of much value bought separately; Collection: Lechler; $3-$8 each.

Figure M-9: waffle toy goblet; clear; 1¼″ tall; Collection: Feltner; $20-$35.

Figure M-10: paneled pressed glass sugar bowl; Collection: Largent; $35-$60.

Figure M-11: ivy bowls in miniature; 2¾″ tall; clear, amber, blue and possibly other colors; Collections: Largent and Lechler; $65-$75.

Figure M-12: syrup in miniature; Collection: Walters; $40-$45.

Figure M-13: Moser pitcher and bowl; emerald green with enamel; possibly goes with matching tumble up and dresser pieces; Collection: Lechler; $100-$125.

Figure M-14: vases; crystal; Collection: Walters; $40-$60 pair.

Figure M-15: bride's basket in miniature; Collection: Welker; $150-$200.

Figure M-16: cheese dish; clear with red and white enamel; Collection: Lechler; $75-$150.

Figure M-17: toy loving cup; Collection: Largent; $18-$30.

Figure M-18: Flattened Diamond (type) tray; Collection: Largent; $70-$80.

CONTEMPORARY TOY GLASS

Figure L-10, Little Jo or Arched Panels: This toy water set was originally produced in clear, light pink, light green and rich amber and was then reproduced in a large variety of colors. Westmoreland began producing the water set again in 1977 for Levay Distribution Co. Five hundred sets were made in purple. In 1979 the sets were made in amberina-red, cobalt, emerald, crystal, red carnival, cobalt, carnival green, and cobalt with hand painted flowers. Levay discontinued the toy sets in 1981. Westmoreland reissued the set in 1983 in crystal as their anniversary offering. The moulds have been purchased by Summit Glass Company and sets were produced in tangerine and cobalt.

Figure TS-31, Lamb: table set first produced in clear glass, then white milkglass; now reoffered in a multitude of colors.

Figure Wetzel 1 and 2: hobnail water sets produced in several colors, some of which are still available; Zanesville, Ohio.

Figure P-10, Thumbelina or Flattened Diamond: punch set; reissued in a large variety of colors.

Figure C-1, three-branch candlesticks: reissued in a large variety of colors such as mother of pearl, cobalt, orange etc.

Figure B-1, reamers: one color every few months from the same mould; by Edna Barnes of Ohio; began 1981; 1,000 made in each color.

Most of Tom Mosser's new toy ware is still available. For more information and ordering, contact: Tom Mosser, Cambridge, Ohio 43725; 614-439-1827.

Figure TM-1, cherry cracker jar (206-6d)

Figure TM-2, cherry berry set (206-4d)

Figure TM-3, cherry butter dish (206-3d)

Figure TM-4, cherry water set (206-1d)

Figure TM-5, cherry goblet (206-7d)

Figure TM-8, cherry spooner (206-2d)

Figure TM-9, Inverted Strawberry punch set

Figure TM-11 and TM-12, cherry sugar and creamer (206-5c)

Figure TM-13, Dutch candlesticks

Figure TM-14, chocolate glass cherry water set

Figure TM-16, green relish Jennifer

Figure TM-17, green sugar, Jennifer

Figure TM-18, green spooner, Jennifer

Figure TM-19, green creamer, Jennifer

Figure TM-20, green divided dish, Jennifer

Figure TM-21, green covered butter, Jennifer

Figure TM-22, green cup, Jennifer

Figure TM-23, green saucer, Jennifer

Figure TM-24, green plate, Jennifer

Figure TM-25, green ice bucket, Jennifer

Figure TM-26, yellow goblet, Jennifer

Figure TM-27, yellow plate, Jennifer

Figure TM-28, yellow plate, Jennifer

Figure TM-29, yellow bowl, Jennifer

Figure TM-30, yellow creamer, Jennifer

Figure TM-31, yellow sugar, Jennifer

Figure TM-32, yellow platter, Jennifer

Figure TM-33, yellow vase

Figure TM-34, pink pitcher, Jennifer

Figure TM-35, pink sherbert, Jennifer

Figure TM-36, pink candlestick, Jennifer

Figure TM-37, pink ice bucket, Jennifer

Figure TM-38, pink mayo, Jennifer

Figure TM-39, pink plate, Jennifer

Figure TM-40, pink plate, Jennifer

Figure TM-41, pink cracker jar, Jennifer

Note: Watch for additional old toy glass which will be featured in *French and German Dolls, Dishes and Accessories* by Doris Anderson Lechler.

LECHLER HEIRLOOMS

Figure LH-6, plain custard tumble up; first of the Lechler series along with an eight piece lemonade set; violets were hand painted on the items later; production started 1980.

Figure LH-5, custard tumble up with hand painted violets.

Figure LH-5, eight piece lemonade set with hand painted violets; the first sets were issued without hand painting.

Figure LH-7, seventy-five custard sets were hand painted with Christmas holly and red ribbon.

Figure LH-2, Burmese glass was used as the second use of the Lechler mould; this was a seven piece set with 500 sets having been produced and sold.

Figure LH-3, the third and last use of the ruffled lemonade set was produced in amethyst, first with hand painted lily-of-the-valley and then with a Louise Piper Victorian design of birds and roses.

Figure LH-14, seventy-five eight piece lemonade sets in amethyst were hand painted with blue birds and roses; this was the last time the ruffled-rim mould was used.

Figure LH-15, cranberry tumble up; second use of this mould was the last because it was too difficult to make; only seventy-five complete tumble ups were produced in cranberry over-lay; there is one more color (use) left for this mould.

Figure LH-9, blue satin cased-glass tumble up; fall of 1982; hand painted with pinks; the tumbler fits inside the neck of the pitcher.

Figure LH-11, cobalt cased-glass tumble up with hand-painted flowers; second use of the LH-9 mould; one more mould use is still available; at times the pitcher, tray and six tumblers were sold to form a little lemonade set.

Figure LH-12, cobalt cased-glass lemonade set with hand-painted flowers.

Figure LH-16, cranberry opalescent hobnail lemonade set sold in services of four or six with accommodating trays in French opalescent.

Figure LH-8, cobalt cased-glass hobnail lemonade set; eight piece set; second use for the moulds.

Figure LH-13, French opalescent eight piece punch set with a chain of hand-painted baby roses and forget-me-nots around the rim of the ruffled punch bowl; each footed cup has a drop rose in the base of the cup.

Figure LH-1, cobalt eight piece punch set with hand painting; second use of the moulds.

Figure LH-10, sample; custard glass with hand-painted pansies and gold trim; painted by Louise Piper.

All Lechler Heirlooms have been sold out for several years.

BIBLIOGRAPHY

Barlow, Raymond, Kaiser, Joan. *A GUIDE TO SANDWICH GLASS, Witch Balls, Containers and Toys.* Barlow-Kaiser Publishing Co. with Schiffer Publishing, 1987.

Florence, Gene. *THE COLLECTOR'S ENCYCLOPEDIA AKRO AGATE GLASSWARE.* Collector Books, 1975.

Heacock, William. *UNITED STATES GLASS FROM A-Z*, Bk 5.

Lechler, Doris; O'Neill, Virginia. *CHILDREN'S GLASS DISHES.* Thomas Nelson, Nashville, Tn., 1976.

Lechler, Doris. *CHILDREN'S GLASS DISHES, CHINA AND FURNITURE.* Collector Books. Paducah, Ky., 1983.

Lechler, Doris. *CHILDREN'S GLASS DISHES, CHINA AND FURNITURE, Vol. II.* Collector Books. Paducah, Ky., 1986.

Lechler, Doris. *MINIATURE NEWS* newsletter publications.

Revi, Christian. *AMERICAN PRESSED GLASS AND FIGURE BOTTLES.* Thomas Nelson, 1972.

Richter, Miriam. *IOWA CITY GLASS.* Des Moines, Iowa. Wallace-Homestead, 1966.

Weatherman, Hazel. *COLORED GLASSWARE OF THE DEPRESSION ERA II.* Weatherman Glass Books. Springfield, Mo., 1974.